The Story of

THE McGUFFEYS

Alexander McGuffey, "Sandy the Scout," father of William Holmes and Alexander Hamilton McGuffey. From a painting by Sewell, Cincinnati, about 1840.

Alice McGuffey Ruggles

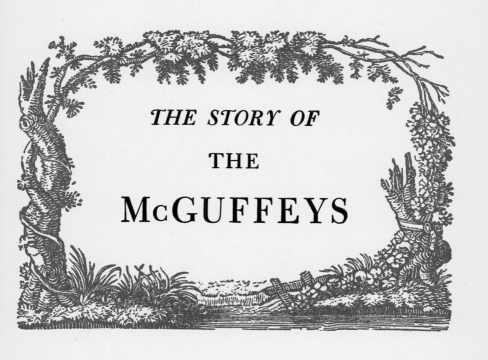

THE STORY OF

THE

McGUFFEYS

American Book Company   NEW YORK   CINCINNATI

CHICAGO   BOSTON   ATLANTA   DALLAS   SAN FRANCISCO

TO THE MEMORY OF

Daniel Blaisdell Ruggles,

WHO ENCOURAGED ME TO WRITE THIS BOOK,

AND TO

Dan Junior and Eleanor

FOREWORD

THIS IS A STORY — not a documented history. The first American McGuffeys were too busy or too illiterate or too lacking in self-consciousness to write of themselves. They left no family records, and firsthand material on their background is scanty. When facts were available, I followed them scrupulously. What traditions I could gather, I handed on. Failing both, I fell back on probabilities — with apologies to my forebears, who seem to have been very matter-of-fact.

Information on the Scottish emigrants, William McGuffey — "Billy" in the story — and his wife, Ann McKittrick, I owe to Mr. George A. Ostheimer of Indiana, whose wife was descended from Catherine, sister of "Sandy the Scout."

Dr. Daniel Drake, one of the first Westerners to develop a sense of the regional history, left an account of the youthful exploits of "Sandy" (the first Alexander McGuffey) told to him by the scout himself. The journal of Dr. Drake's brother, Benjamin, and certain Drake letters give glimpses of young Alexander Hamilton McGuffey, who collaborated in the compilation of the *Readers*. And the unpublished autobiography of Charles D. Drake, the doctor's son, contains vivid pictures of life in southern Ohio in the early nineteenth century.

A sketch of Dr. Henry McGuffey of Kentucky, who was the baby on the horseback trek of Sandy and Anna to northern Ohio in 1802, was written for me by Miss Jennie McGuffey of Seattle, the doctor's granddaughter.

vii

Miss Katherine Walker Stewart of Dayton, last surviving grandchild of William Holmes McGuffey, turned over to me her collection of family photographs and papers. And from her lips I wrote down her own recollections of her maternal grandfather and his second wife, Laura Howard. The description she gave me of William's earlier married life with his first wife, Harriet Spining, she had received from her mother, Mary McGuffey Stewart.

In my interview with my cousin Katherine she urged me, in whatever I might publish about the *Readers*, to bring out the *human* side of the story. For many years she had been meeting McGuffey devotees who paid tribute to her as a granddaughter of the educator but knew little about the real personalities behind their beloved old schoolbooks.

Of Alexander Hamilton McGuffey in his later years, I have my own recollections. He was the indulgent grandfather *par excellence*, associated with trips, treats, and marvelous Christmas parties under his hospitable roof. For his earlier married life with Elizabeth Drake, the grandmother I never knew, I have used the recollections of my mother, Anna McGuffey Morrill.

Secondary sources, mostly articles in magazines and newspapers, are too numerous to list. Two invaluable books of reference are *A History of the McGuffey Readers* by Henry M. Vail, written from the publisher's angle, and *William Holmes McGuffey and His Readers* by Dr. Harvey C. Minnich.

My aim in this little volume has been to make these old-fashioned Americans and their world come to life.

The Story of

THE McGUFFEYS

I

THE MCGUFFEYS (or MacGuffies) must have belonged
originally to the great clan of the fighting MacFies who
ranged the mountains of northwestern Scotland. But by
the eighteenth century they had long since drifted to the
south and become Lowland farmers and artisans, law-
abiding, industrious, and ardent in the faith of the Covenanters.

Outwardly tamed, they kept their proud independence
of spirit, and a gnawing restlessness tormented them within.
But they lived their hard lives of work and prayer uncomplainingly, and even found a kind of savor in the hardness.

Wigtownshire, where they settled, is the bleak jut of
bog and moorland that separates the Irish Sea and the
North Channel. Here, under gray skies with foggy salt
air blowing in from the hundreds of bays that dent the
shore ("viks" in the days of the Norsemen, corrupted to
"wigs"), generations of McGuffeys grew up to lives
seemingly narrow and monotonous. Actually, within their

I

cottages, little dramas of agonized birth, difficult living, and cruel dying were endlessly being played.

Their land and their religion were rich with dark background, glorious memories of bloody suffering and stern survival.

The mothers sang as they rocked the cradles a song that harked back to the fourteenth century, when Wigtownshire had been callously handed over for a bad debt by the earl who owned it to one of the terrible "Black Douglases," Archibald the Grim:

Hush ye, hush ye, little pet-ye,
Hush ye, hush ye, dinna fret ye,
The Black Douglas shall na get ye!

In the gloom of the long winter evenings, when families huddled close together by the smoldering peat fires, the old grandsires would make the youngsters' flesh creep with tales of the Covenanter martyrs.

On this very Wigtown beach, where the children romped and gathered kelp and their fathers launched their fishing boats, a widow of sixty-four and a young girl of eighteen had been lashed to stakes in the sand and left to drown because they would not renounce their faith. On the hill beyond the town where now the children went to watch the ships in the harbor, gibbets had stood and bodies of steadfast Covenanter men had swung to and fro, rotting in the wind and fog.

The Lord had suffered these things to be. But not in vain. At long last the wicked Stuart kings had been driven across the seas, exiled to France.

2

Once since, their driddling Pretender had nearly landed on Wigtown beach. Three warships had been blown up in that affair, and good men killed. But the attempt had come to nothing. And soon after, the hated bishops, too, had been forced to leave Scotland. Thenceforth and forever a Covenanter might worship God in the way he held good, without priests or pomp.

Thrilling these old tales were, but there came a day when the young found more intriguing certain present troubles, of which their parents whispered among themselves. Something threatened their daily life, something less clearly to be pictured than drownings, hangings, and battles. The children saw it as a mysterious specter that stalked the moors at night, laying deathly hands upon the beggars and tramps they saw lying stricken in the ditches.

At night in the one-room cottages, pretending to be sound asleep, they overheard sad talk. "We live in terrible times . . . soon there will be no meal nor milk to fill the little bellies . . . no clothing to cover their nakedness, nor wood to keep them warm. . . . Scrimp as we may, we poor are growing poorer and the rich richer. . . . God help us, we freeholders may become slaves of the landlords or vagabonds on the road."

All this was true. The yeoman class, to which the McGuffeys belonged, was being ruined by the newfangled methods of farming brought over from France and Holland, which only the upper classes could afford to apply. Gentlemen of leisure were taking up farming for diversion and profit, and humble folk had to work for them as virtual serfs.

The infamous "Inclosure Acts" took from the poor man his "Commons," where from time immemorial he had raised his potatoes, pastured his cows and pigs, and cut his firewood, rights which had made all the difference between scanty living and starvation. Facing ruin, some farmers found work in the newly-opened factories with long hours and wretched pay. Some took to the road and lapsed into beggary and crime. Those who could scrape up the price of the passage migrated with their families to Ireland, Canada, or the colonies.

II

OUT OF THIS SHADOWY past emerges a certain angular individual named Billy McGuffey, a man who attended
strictly to his own business, farming and cobbling, and
to his religion, a rigid uncompromising Calvinism. He
was unsociable, mingling intimately only with his kith and
kin. Quick and generous to help a neighbor in trouble, he
preferred not to be thanked. He hated to be contradicted,
and no one would have dared to lay a hand upon him in
restraint. He adored his wife, Ann, but tried to cage her
spirit with his own iron will.

Billy was educated; he wrote a fine hand and read all the
books he could get. He was pious, and he was canny.
While others went about lamenting the poverty-stricken
times and quoting Scripture, Billy kept his mind on ways
and means. He had a saying, "What maun be, can be." He
would emigrate.

Of his wife, Ann (born McKittrick), we know only
that she had courage and that her husband's word was,

5

after the Bible, her law. She knew her Bible only through
the minister's reading in the kirk, or Billy's, for she could
neither read nor write. But she could think and understand
and work. She patched the threadbare clothing over and
over, stinted the porridge, and doled out the wood and
peat. Slowly the pennies accumulated in the old sack behind the chimney.

In the spring of 1774, very cautiously, Billy and Ann
began to make their plans to leave. He was thirty-two, she
twenty-seven. Their children were a boy of seven, Alexander, and two little girls of six and four, Catherine and
Elizabeth.

The small brig in which they sailed took the best part
of three months to reach Philadelphia. The weather held
good, but to Ann the crossing was a long-drawn-out nightmare.

Supplies of food, often rancid or spoiled, were issued
once a week and cooked by the passengers over fires in an
open galley. The sleeping bunks were mere shelves of
rough boards, lining the hold in tiers of three. Billy and
Sandy slept together in a lower bunk, Ann and the two
little girls in one above them. Many of the emigrants slept
on the floor, where rats and cockroaches scampered about
when the oil lamps were turned low. The air of the hold
reeked with mingled smells of cooking, bilge water, and
human effluvia. Passengers brought along their own bedding, and Ann's spotless blankets were soon crawling. The
Scottish girl began to believe that though she had been
poor all her life, in such matters as cleanliness and fresh
air she had lived like a queen.

6

A Scottish village in Billy McGuffey's youth.

A Scottish Lowland town in 1793.

High Street, Philadelphia, with the First Presbyterian Church, at about the time Billy and Ann arrived there.

Philadelphia: The bridge over Front Street at Arch, in colonial days.

trouble-making Indians. Reconnoitering along the banks of the Big and Little Captina creeks, with Captain Boggs leading the way on a fine white horse, they could find "nary hair nor hide of a redskin." But they woke on the fifth morning to find fresh footprints on the fringes of the camp. Indians had been watching them as they slept and were probably watching now from the bushes.

Captain Boggs ordered the soldiers to untether their horses and mount, and, again himself conspicuously leading the way, all rode cautiously up and down the thickly-wooded banks of the creek. Sandy and Duncan, on foot, their fingers twitching on their cocked guns, crept in and out of the undergrowth, searching, listening.

Suddenly a volley cracked from the bushes. The captain groaned, toppled, and slid from his saddle.

Sandy and Duncan made for a large sycamore and, crouching behind the trunk, fired into the bushes, Sandy eight or ten times. The Indians fired back, and one of the bullets knocked some of the sycamore bark into Duncan's face. Duncan, reloading, cool and imperturbable, remarked, "Didn't the fellow fire well?"

The soldiers had come galloping up behind their captain, and three of them fell from their horses, wounded. Now the Indians rushed out from their ambush, and the scouts had to flee for their lives.

Duncan was chased down the creek by five Indians, while Sandy ran up a hill with three more after him. Reaching the top, he wheeled suddenly and pointed his empty gun at them. The old trick served. The enemy instantly dropped into the grass, and Sandy tore away into the woods and reached the settlement half an hour before Duncan, who as usual turned up without a scratch. The luck of these two was proverbial.

The same afternoon a party went back with a larger force to the scene of the skirmish. The Indians had vanished, but the crumpled body of Captain Boggs lay where he had fallen, riddled with five bullets. His men dug a grave and buried him on the spot. To this day the people of that region tell of the bloody "Battle of the Captinas" and the gallant officer who rode ahead of his men and received the first charge of the attack, like a living target.

In the thicket Sandy discovered traces of blood and, a few days later, the freshly-buried bodies of the three Indians, those he and Duncan had shot from behind the sycamore.

Years later, when the Indian wars were over, a big Indian came up to Sandy in Wheeling and told him there had been forty Indians against the whites in the Battle of the Captinas; that is, more than three to one.

He added, holding out his hand, "And I was one of the three who chased you up the hill."

Sandy shook his hand and suggested they have a foot race. This they did, before a gallery of whites and Indians, and Sandy won. The big Indian gravely asked to shake his hand again.

In the fall of 1791 Sandy and Duncan shared in the unlucky campaign of General Arthur St. Clair, the erratic British officer, who had been highly praised at the beginning of the Revolution for throwing in his lot with the colonists and hotly criticized later for surrendering Fort

Ticonderoga to Burgoyne. Now he was Governor of the Northwest Territory, and President Washington had given him orders to clear up the Indian situation for good and all.

Through the summer of '91 St. Clair wrestled getting his expedition under way. He was fifty-four and might have excused himself from commanding in person on the score of his administrative duties as well as of age. But, being Scottish, he liked to run everything himself.

He had planned to start in July, but it was autumn when he finally set out from Fort Washington for the Maumee country, with two thousand recruits collected in Pennsylvania and Kentucky. It was the devil's job to raise troops in the New West, the militia and the volunteers were so touchy, independent, and jealous of each other.

Sam Brady with Sandy and Duncan was detailed to reconnoiter along the Great Lakes. Neither of the younger men had ever been so far north before. Brady told them to bring along their dogs.

The march through the unbroken wilderness was an agony. Water was scarce, and food as well, after the supply of jerked venison and parched corn began to run low. They dared not hunt for springs nor shoot game. The woods were alive with Indians, who through their own spies knew all about General St. Clair's plans and were in a most dangerous mood.

Brady's party traveled at night and by day lay hidden in the forest, snatching what sleep they could. At last, exhausted, their clothes half torn off by briars and branches, their throats parched, they staggered out into the open of a swamp on the shore of Lake Erie, and Brady guided their footsteps to a beautiful fountain-like spring. They drank eagerly, bathed in the cool, delicious water, and lay down in the deep sedges to rest. The pure air from the Great Lakes blew over them like the breath of Heaven. But it was Hell, not Paradise they had reached.

Brady was tense and anxious. When Sandy asked if he knew whereabouts they were lying, he muttered grimly, "Ay, I know well enough — nigh here they burned Crawford."

That did not make a man feel good.

Nine years before, Colonel William Crawford had been sent north from Fort Pitt to fight the Delawares and Wyandots and had been defeated and captured near the present site of the city of Sandusky. All one day from sunrise to sunset the savages had slowly tortured him while the white renegade Simon Girty stood by, deaf to his anguished appeals.

They tied Crawford up, blackened his face, stripped him naked, cut off his ears, and shot his body full of black powder. They made him "run the gauntlet," burned holes in his flesh with fiery sticks, threw baskets of hot coals in his face, and drove him barefoot over the hot ashes of the fire at the stake. When they were surfeited and he had fallen, fainting, into the fire, they tomahawked him and burned him up.

This affair had horrified the entire frontier. "Avenge Crawford!" was the slogan on every expedition that set out against the Indians after his death.

The thought that they were lying near the scene of Crawford's torture sent a shudder down Sandy's spine.

The Indians pouring into the woods not fifty yards away were members of the same cruel tribes. He and his friends were virtually surrounded; the slightest movement might betray them. With his left hand Sandy stroked the warm, skinny body of his beloved Jock, who lay in the curve of his arm. With his right he gripped his trusty rifle. The moment of panic passed. But none of the party slept that day.

At dusk Brady gave the order to turn back. Sleep or no sleep, food or no food, they must go back and warn St. Clair. The Indian forces were overwhelming, and it would be crazy to join battle without heavy reinforcements. By now the general should have reached the upper Maumee (near the present city of Fort Wayne). They must strike off to the southwest to intercept him.

The men ate their last handfuls of corn and dried meat, feeding shreds to the famished dogs. Their food pouches were empty, and a two-day journey, at quickest, lay before them over wild, unbroken ground.

All that night they marched, but the next day lay hidden in the brush. Each took his turn at watching while the others snatched a little sleep. The fires of the Indian camps were all about them. They found a few wild berries for food and drink. At night they stumbled on. On the second morning, Brady said the dogs must be killed for food.

Sandy drew his knife and threw it at the leader's feet.

"Can't do it with a knife," whispered Brady, "they would yell. Their throats — choke them with your long fingers, McGuffey. And be quick about it! Damme," for Sandy made no move, "we must eat if we are to march. What are ye? Soldier, or milksop?"

"We be Scotch Covenanters, — can do what we must," muttered Sandy hoarsely. With a face like thunder he stepped forward and very tenderly lifted Jock in his arms, motioning Duncan to take up Meggie.

The younger man obeyed, and the two disappeared into the thicket. They ate their dogs. But Sandy and Duncan would never discuss the subject as long as they lived.

Covering forty miles the last night, the scouts arrived at St. Clair's headquarters, haggard and famished. Brady made his report.

The general listened impatiently, told the scout he was an alarmist, and gave his troops the orders to march on. What happened is history.

Trapped on a hill between a ravine and a creek, the whites were attacked, as the scouts had foreseen, from ambush on every side and were beaten to a finish in the bloodiest battle in all the annals of the frontier.

The retreat was a rout. Indians appeared from behind every tree, howling like fiends. Like fiends, the whites fought back. Most of the officers were killed, and half the men. Hundreds fled singly all over the wilderness and were cut down, scalped, or dragged away as prisoners never to be seen again.

A few stragglers reached Fort Washington to tell the wretched tale. St. Clair, ill and crippled, was lifted on a horse and ignominiously led along. He resigned, and the President appointed General Wayne, "Mad Anthony," to take his place.

By some miracle Sandy and Duncan escaped unharmed and cut across country to Logtown, ten miles above

Wheeling, and thence home. The sacrifice of their dogs was a small part of what they had suffered, but it seemed to rankle most.

Wayne took two years to train his troops in every phase of Indian warfare. At last he led them, skilled and disciplined and accompanied by a small army of scouts and spies, to join battle near the scene of St. Clair's defeat, and beyond. In August, 1794, at the Battle of Fallen Timbers, he gave the Indians their *coup de grace*. They were cut down and defeated forever. The Treaty of Greenville, signed a year later, inaugurated a lasting peace. The Ohio country was safe from the redskins, and settlers could give their attention solely to the problems of living.

Sandy and Duncan came back from the wars, hung up their rifles over their fathers' chimneys, and asked themselves, "What now?"

VI

THEY KNEW WELL ENOUGH what they must do. A man couldn't keep on hunting and fighting forever. Lasses needed husbands, and men had to have children to carry on the work they had begun.

A frontier wife should be strong and handy in the housework, and comeliness was enjoyable through long winter evenings. And a Covenanter's wife must be pious and good, as well.

Catherine McGuffey had married a middle-aged farmer, a veteran of the Revolution, and left home. Sandy found it dull at home with his elderly parents. William was fifty-two, Ann forty-seven, but she seemed older.

Duncan was courting Nancy, the pretty sister of his friend John McDonald, another Scotsman who had been a scout in the Ohio country. All of a sudden Sandy began to take notice of Anna Holmes. He had known her ever since he came West. She had grown up now, and he saw her with different eyes.

Anna's father, Henry Holmes, owned "Rural Grove," the largest farm in the county. His four hundred acres lay two and a half miles away from the McGuffey place. His cabin had two stories. Few settlers had more than two or three books on their cupboard shelves. Holmes had six. He was English; his wife, Jane, born Roney, was Irish; and they had been married in Ireland. Jane's brother, Hercules, had come out with them to the West, a giant of a man, like his name for strength, and a terror in the Indian wars.

Anna had crisp chestnut hair, blue-gray eyes, a nose tilted like a morning-glory. Her laughter was a chime of bells, loud and joyous. She came into a cabin like a spring freshet, sweeping all before her. She was serious, too, and keen for reading. She kept her suitors guessing.

Sandy fell in love the day he went over to "Rural Grove" on an errand, a day like any other day. But there stood Anna, tall and willowy in the sunlight by the cabin door, holding a brown puppy to her shoulder as though it were a baby. There were five other puppies in the barn. Would Sandy like one, she asked him, smiling radiantly.

No, he answered shortly, he would never own a dog again. The quick tears filled Anna's eyes, and she turned away into the cabin to call her mother. Everyone knew what had happened to Sandy's Jock.

How kind she was and how bonny! From that hour Sandy saw her tender shining eyes by day and by night, smiling, weeping for him. "Ann-a! Ann-a!" the name rang in his ears. His mother's name, but lighter, sweeter than plain Ann. His wooing was shy but intense. He talked little, but he gave Anna no peace.

They were married at "Rural Grove" just before Christmas, 1797. Not that Christmas meant anything to Covenanters. But it was a convenient season for weddings on the frontier. Work was slack. Why not get married?

All morning the guests came galloping through the frosty woods, tethered and covered their horses, and, crowding into the roomy cabin, warmed themselves around the great roaring fire.

The ceremony was at noon. The bride wore a thistle-colored gown of linsey-woolsey with a kerchief of snowy white folded about her slender neck and crossed between her breasts. Sandy had got him a new doeskin smock. Anna spoke her answers loud and clear, but the groom's tongue clove to the roof of his mouth.

After the service the guests shook Sandy's hand and clapped him thunderously on the back, embraced the bride and wished her well. A silence fell when the minister raised his hand and asked a blessing on the food. Then voraciously the company fell upon the mountains of smoking victuals Jane Holmes and her helpers had set out on long trestle tables against the walls. Reserves of food simmered on the hearth or over the fire. Roast venison, wild turkey, vegetables, fruit sauces, johnnycake with maple syrup or honey, wonders (the frontier brand of crullers), all to be washed down with jugs of milk, cider, and sweetened water.

These people had come from countries where food was scarce. In the New West, though living was rough and luxuries few, the settlers never felt that lack. And in the Covenanters' strict catechism there was nothing against

33

indulgence in food. At weddings they ate until they were gorged, sat about for hours, and ate again.

Towards evening the company mounted horses or climbed into wagons and proceeded to Billy McGuffey's place, where Ann and her daughter Catherine served another enormous meal. Sandy and Anna were to make their home at "Rural Grove." So later in the evening the younger guests and the Holmes family escorted them back for the final festivities, "the infare."

The fire was built up, the lard lamps trimmed, and they played games and practical jokes. Uncle Hercules Roney got out the old fiddle he had brought from Ulster for square dancing. The girls and boys pressed hands discreetly as the figures changed.

At midnight, apples and wonders and cider were passed around for the last time. The crowning moment of the infare had arrived. Candles were lighted by the women in the upper story, and the big bed was warmed; and Sandy carried his tall bride up the ladder, her flaming cheeks hidden in her husband's shoulder. The trap door closed with a bang.

In less sober circles this would have been the signal for a wild outburst of carousing and noise, of cheers and jeers, of horseplay and the beating of iron kettles until daybreak. But Covenanters had more delicate manners.

The guests began to leave by twos and threes, clattering down the road in the cold starlight, their laughter and singing restrained to proper bounds. The outer and the inner man had been well satisfied, and the frontier talked of that wedding for years.

In three years Anna had presented Sandy with three children — a daughter and two sons, born in their little sloping-roofed room under the eaves at "Rural Grove."

Anna named her first child Jane for her mother. The next, a son, Sandy said must be called William for his father. But Anna slipped in Holmes for the middle name, just in case she never had another son. When a second boy appeared she gave him the full name of her father, Henry Holmes, who was so generous to all. "Rural Grove" overflowed with his own offspring and the five McGuffeys.

William Holmes McGuffey was a precocious child. At birth he had been a plain-faced infant with a wide mouth, like a young robin's, a little plum nose, and a solemn expression. But his eyes redeemed all, large and dark, beautiful and searching. From the first Anna felt he was destined to rise in the world. At two he was a strong well-grown child, self-contained, observant, and capable. Jane and Henry were healthy and pleasant, but William was different. His mother pinned her hopes to him.

Sandy, the father, was growing pioneer-restless. He wanted land of his own and something harder to "wrastle with" than the tilling of his father-in-law's prosperous farm. "Push out! Push out!" the harrow seemed to say as he thrust it along the rows with his big-boned hands.

Duncan McArthur had married his Nancy and taken her away to the Ohio country, where he had bought a tract of fertile land on the Scioto River near the newly-founded village of Chillicothe. He told Sandy those who had fought to make the land safe for settling should get their pick while it was going cheap.

Duncan was always canny. He had picked up a knowledge of surveying and got a job as chainman between seasons of scouting. Now he began to acquire property by shrewd buying and by locating land warrants that were issued to Revolutionary soldiers. By 1804, nine years after he had gone to Ohio, he was rated the wealthiest landholder in his county, a rising man with an eye to the future.

Sandy broke it to Anna that he was hankering to move up north to a far wilder part than Duncan's Scioto country. Up where you could get more for your money. Anna was willing. "Whither thou goest, I will go, and where thou lodgest, I will lodge." But she knew it was the freedom of the wilderness that attracted Sandy more than the price.

He bought one hundred and sixty acres for five hundred dollars on the long-time contract plan. Fourteen years of grinding work he and Anna put in on that land before they received their deed.

For the young wife it was hard to leave the comparative comforts of western "Penn" and her relatives and friends. Since her people had first come over the mountains, log schoolhouses and churches had been built, and corduroy roads. But where she was going there were no roads, no public buildings of any kind. In the unbroken wilderness she and Sandy would have to begin at the beginning, as their forebears had done — with what struggles she knew only too well.

Sandy's mother, Ann, thought a great pother was being made over this migration. She had been only two years older than Anna when she crossed the ocean with her three bairns and not much more than the clothes on their backs. Now this fine young lady must take with her this, that, and the other to the raw North. In the end most of Anna's gear had to be left behind, for the present. A wagon was out of the question, Sandy said. He knew that country; he had followed Sam Brady through it on hands and knees often enough.

His father gave him a horse, and Henry Holmes gave Anna an old white mare. As parting gifts for his grandchildren Billy McGuffey made each one a pair of shoes. He could still make better shoes than could be bought at Wheeling or Pitt. For little Henry, the youngest, he whittled a wooden rattle, a miniature of the one he had shaken to scare the crows with when he was a child in Scotland.

He had been barely five when he had begun to work at crow-scaring for the neighboring farmers. A penny a day he had been paid, a working day that stretched from dawn until dark, and how glad his parents had been to get those pennies! Of those bad old days across the water he and Ann never talked at all.

Billy had a gift for trading land. He went here and there along the frontier buying and selling parcels, making a dollar out of anything he touched. Ann at home had not to worry about money any more. In the late afternoon she took her ease, sitting in the mild weather with her knitting on the bench outside the cabin door, wearing a good "stuff" gown and a spotless apron. The settlement was a busy place now.

It was good not to have to move again — so many of their neighbors, shiftless or restless, were forever moving on, further west or north — good to have a fence around the dooryard and leisure to tend a few flowers there.

Always the pioneer women yearned for gardens, but flowers were the last thing a housewife had time to cultivate. Besides, what was the use when the men were always uprooting their families and dragging them off to another clearing or a bigger cabin, and the straggling little rows of cherished flowers had to be left behind?

Ann McGuffey pored over her flowers as though they were books, studying their ways as she pulled away the weeds with twisted workworn fingers or cut a handful to stick in an earthen jar on the window ledge. Her hens and geese she talked to as if they were people.

On the summer morning that Sandy and Anna were to start north, she got up at dawn to cut a fine nosegay of cockscombs, four-o'clocks, gillyflowers, and balsam, and she and Billy walked over to "Rural Grove." Covenanters were not demonstrative, but Anna threw both arms around her mother-in-law's neck and kissed her cheeks, hard and brown as russet apples. Little Jane stuck the nosegay in the bridle of the old white mare that was taking them to the new home.

Anna rode the mare on a broad pack saddle, her baby Henry in her arms, with Jane and William in paniers on either side. In a smaller basket lay a pudgy brown puppy, descendant of the one Anna had been holding the day Sandy fell in love.

A second horse followed them, loaded with clothing, bedding, tools, and kitchen utensils. The progress was necessarily slow.

Campus Martius, the stockaded fort built at
Marietta in 1791.

Fort Washington in 1790.

Immigrants descending the Ohio on a flatboat.

Border settlers in Ohio putting up a cabin.

A settler's home in the Northwest Territory.

Making the westward trek to Ohio in 1805.

Part of the remains of Fort Pitt, January, 1834.

The Battle of Fallen Timbers, August, 1794.

Sandy walked ahead, leading the horses single file, hauling the mare forward by main force when she stuck between the close-growing trees.

Jane McGuffey was old enough to remember this journey all her life. At noon the mother handed out thick sandwiches across the mare's back. They cooked their supper by the side of a brook and fell asleep to the sound of rippling water. It was their mother who said the blessing over the food and led in singing hymns, their mother's laughter that rang out echoing through the forest when the horses balked or the bundles caught in the bushes. But it was their father who got them through.

As they neared their journey's end a sudden storm broke, one of the near-tornadoes of the Ohio country. Thunder rolled, and the trail and streams ran roaring.

Sandy left the family at a cabin in the settlement of Youngstown and pushed on with a guide to the edge of his claim. He had a wish to see his own trees before he slept. By the time they reached the place where stakes and notches were visible, the storm had passed over and the sun filtered into the clearing. Sandy stood a while gazing intently into the depths of his own forest.

As scout and hunter, how he had loved the black fastnesses, the thick trunks and encircling boughs — the mystery, solitude, and security, the strange friendliness of it all. Now the trees had become enemies that he must destroy or bend to his needs. He must have space for his house and fields and pastures, wood for building and fuel. He must clear roads and make bridges across rivers so that Anna could get to church and the young ones to school in the villages that would soon be spreading in the wilderness. Instead of the Indians he would have wild animals, droughts, and pests to fight. But his first attack must be on the solid forest. He began the next day.

The old fierce fighting look came into his eyes as he girdled the trees and set fire to the brush. With his own hands he laid out a road to Youngstown. "McGuffey's Road" is his monument today.

After a long day in the field, he would work on late into the night on his road building, and come home numb and staggering with fatigue, his face grim, his hands trembling from his digging and hauling. Anna would feed him, and he would tumble into bed without a word. She never told him he had undertaken too much. She knew that in the morning his toughened body would be as fresh as ever.

Anna was ambitious. The road *had* to be made, the road that would lead her children to education, to power and position, the road to the future.

VII

ANNA HOLMES HAD BEEN twenty-one when she married Sandy McGuffey. She was twenty-five when they moved to Ohio. Five more children were born to them there, four daughters and a son. Their names were Anna, Catherine, Elizabeth, Alexander, and Asenath. Withindoors Anna ruled with a rod of iron sheathed in velvet. From her Irish mother she had her warm heart and her quick temper, hot and dangerous and over in a flash, and from her father a will that brooked no resistance.

"You must do as I say," was her constant rule. If a child talked back, "But *why* must I, Ma?" the answer might be a smile, an embrace, or a swift blow, but no argument. She had no time for that. But at bedtime she prayed with her children, taught them and admonished them.

She was deeply pious, and her religion was to be used, not kept for church and Sabbath. If she wanted something, she knelt down and prayed for it; and if it was right for her, God would give it. He was her Heavenly Father, wise and kind and devoted to His child.

The sterner doctrines of Calvin, Anna simply ignored. Predestination to sin, hell-fire, damnation of unbaptized infants — what could such ideas mean to her whose heart was a living spring of happiness and who was busy from morning till night working for those she loved? When the crops failed or the roof caved in or the children had the fever, Sandy marveled at her courage.

"Nay, but whatever comes, there is something bubbles up in *here*," she would say, pressing her hand to her breast.

She had a passion for perfection and cultivated neatness and order in her house with furor. "Thorough cleaning-day" was a time of storm and stress. Sandy, returning from the fields with his sons, would whisper, "Easy now, your mother's on the warpath today."

Anna could spin and weave, and patch and darn and turn the cloth most skillfully. When Sandy ventured to suggest she spare herself, she would quote with a gleam in her eyes, "Whatsoever cometh unto thy hand to do, do it with thy might!" Anna knew her Bible from cover to cover, and texts rang in her ears and rose to her lips unbidden. The words gave her not only inspiration and comfort but the poetry and music her life lacked.

Cleanliness and efficiency were not all she craved. She adored natural beauty and would stop in her scrubbing or churning to gaze out at the sky. Flying clouds and the whipping bare branches of the trees in winter gave her a thrill as keen as the first spring beauty or the early blue-bird's song.

Anna's daughters helped her in the house. But she dwarfed them with her strong personality and amazed them with her gusty moods.

"Jane! Jane! Come *quick!*" she might call suddenly from the dooryard, and her eldest would come racing in panic, a dishrag in her hand.

"Look! My day-lilies! Just opened!" Anna's eyes would be misty with pleasure.

"Pity's sake, Ma, I thought the barn must be on fire," Jane would mutter, annoyed that her heart was thumping, and all for nothing.

"But aren't they ex-*quis*-ite?" Anna liked to use high-faluting words, though her son William said she did not always say them right.

Anna's garden was her outlet. During the first difficult years in the North she had had nothing like that. There had been too much useful work for her to more than dream of fancy doings like flower gardening. But as the years passed Sandy found time to fence in a space before the house where a silver maple tree gave shade on hot summer afternoons. Under the green boughs that swept to the ground like a tent, he made a rustic seat, and here Anna loved to rest after the early noon dinner and again in the twilight.

Along the fence in a narrow border grew her garden flowers, raised from seed her mother sent her. Anna tended these as vigorously as children. But she loved equally the wild flowers that she made the boys bring in from the woods and plant round the roots of the maple: bloodroot, anemones, waxy May apples, sturdy ferns, and violets —

43

purple, white, and yellow. These needed no care, they were self-reliant; she admired them for that. How much their unfolding meant to her, spring after spring, nerve-racked as she was by the long shut-in winter, no one but Anna ever knew.

Behind the barn clever William built a birdhouse, and a pair of bluebirds nested there every spring. When they flew away in the fall, Anna's heart flew with them. "O had I the wings of a dove . . ." But it was not the rest she craved, it was to be out and away, seeing the world, learning new ways to work for the greater glory of God.

No matter what came or went, nor how the housework piled up, in season and out, Anna took time to give her children their first lessons in reading and ciphering, usually at night. In winter, by the dim light of a pine chip or the flickering fire, the children might be limp with sleepiness, but not Anna. Teaching waked her up. She loved to explain and exhort. The letters and figures drawn in the clean ashes must be erased a score of times until they were absolutely perfect.

VIII

But how little, how pitifully little she knew. She told herself it should be different for her children. By hook or by crook they should be educated, above all, William. What a mind — he ate up knowledge, and his memory was prodigious. He needed only to read over a passage once to have it by heart.

When Anna had taught William and Jane all she knew, she urged their father on with his road building so that the children could walk to Youngstown and attend a small school opened by a Presbyterian minister, the Reverend Mr. Wick. The Wicks were from Long Island, English by descent, well-educated and enterprising.

How strange and wise the ways of Providence, reflected Anna. Here were her children receiving instruction from a pious and learned gentleman. If she had been a wealthy lady in Philadelphia she could not have given them better than this. They were learning not only to read and write, but to speak properly — say *cow*, not *ke-ow*; *catch*, not *ketch; creature,* not *critter.* And to drop their voices, not call and shout as she and Sandy did.

Anna strove to correct her own mistakes, but it was almost hopeless. As for Sandy, he would not try at all. And at table he went on shoveling in his food with his knife and chumping loudly, to the sore affliction of his daughter Jane, who could eat as nicely with her two-tined fork from her wooden trencher as the gentry could from pewter with silver.

When winter came and the road was muddy and the afternoons short and stormy, it was arranged that Jane and William should board at the minister's house, returning home for week ends.

How far Jane progressed we do not know, but the clergyman confirmed all that Anna had told him about William's ability and, to the intense delight of both William and his mother, began to teach the lad Latin, in those days the hallmark of learning as distinguished from mere education. He lent William books and put him on the track of borrowing others. The lad would tramp miles to get one and sit up half the night reading, trying to commit the contents to memory before he returned it. With books so scarce, the faculty of memorizing was a help, but William's was no mechanical mind. From the days when he first discussed the Bible at his mother's knee he had always had a questioning, argumentative turn of mind.

William studied with Mr. Wick until he was fifteen or sixteen. Then his teacher gave him a certificate and advised him to become a roving teacher. Sandy McGuffey had other children coming along fast. Henry, the second son, was a bright lad, saving his farm wages and asking for an education; and the girls must have a little learning, too. It was time for William to get out and earn. Of course he would have to return summers and help his father on the farm.

No organized schools existed in the West until 1825. When William set out, he was one of an army of half-educated young men who tramped the roads and trails, drumming up "subscription scholars." If a sufficient number offered and there was a cabin available, he gathered them in and taught them as long as their parents' interest and money held out. It was discouraging work; the parents were for the most part very ignorant and indifferent, the children wild and unruly.

William had grown into a tall, broad-shouldered youth with tough muscles and a rough-hewn, honest face. His forehead was high and broad, his eyes piercing, his nose prominent. His large mouth was set in determined lines but was kind and genial when he could be made to smile.

For so young a man he gave a remarkable impression of brains and character. No one ever forgot him. His most marked trait was his concentration. He had set his mind on certain definite goals for a career, and he never swerved from them. He was sincerely religious and, unknown to anyone but his mother, had determined to become a Presbyterian minister. But his aims went far beyond a country parish. He meant to educate as well as preach. In later life he had a favorite saying, "Light comes from above." He had no particular faith in the ignorant masses. He believed in producing an intelligentsia, the elect, who should lead

47

the people. He had no evangelical passion for saving souls. He figured that if people's minds were enlightened and enriched, they would *want* to do right. And above all begin with the young, the younger the better.

Back and forth he tramped the frontier, in his weather-beaten homespun and patched shoes, shabby but always neat and "respectable," through Ohio, western Pennsylvania, and Kentucky, begging a ride when he could, eating what was given him, teaching whenever he got the chance. In the cabins where he lodged he talked little but complained never. The older people respected him, and the children liked him. He was a strict disciplinarian, but he made the lessons clear and interesting. He was so terribly in earnest about their learning. The older ringleaders in mischief among the boys he thrashed roundly at the beginning of the term, the pert older girls he subdued by glowering at them. If that failed, he expelled them.

All his life he was to bear the marks of these starved years. He had always been serious; now he lost the capacity for pleasure of a lighter kind.

He was naturally shy and too studious to have much in common with the average young frontiersman. As for girls, he put them out of his life as resolutely as though he were a candidate for the priesthood. Not without inner conflicts.

His mother was his only confidante. It angered him when he returned home from his wanderings to find her slaving in the bare farmhouse without comforts or leisure. She herself never complained. Fretting was a fault explicitly forbidden by her faith. Nor could she bear to have him pity her. "Son, I am blessed to have work to do, and the strength to do it. Let me hear no more of that."

His father, too, worked uncomplainingly in the fields or barn and at night sat snoring in the chimney corner, too dog-tired to read or engage in edifying conversation such as William craved. He vowed to himself he would never let himself lapse back into yeomanry. He worked hard on the farm when he was there, but he loathed it.

On his travels a passionate desire had been rising in his heart as he observed the ignorance and mental vacancy of the backwoods people. Crowded ten or twelve in a cabin, they were yet lonely and hungry for something beyond their daily grind. They needed books and teaching, something to feed their souls. William resolved to help them. But first he must get more schooling himself. Nights, after his father and the other children had gone to bed, William and his mother sat alone together, talking over ways and means.

Sandy McGuffey never stayed awake a night in his life, but Anna often lay sleepless for hours scheming how William was to get his training for the ministry. It was a tremendous undertaking. Yet Anna always hitched her wagon to a star.

Her husband was not really interested. Why all this to-do over "larnin'," the genial farmer wondered. Books made his head ache. Still, he was willing to spare William from the farm. Had not his own father spared him for scouting? But so much education cost money, and where was he to lay his hands on cash to send William away to fitting school? After that would come college, and then

49

theological training. Sandy's seventh child had appeared, and he was building a larger house. No, he could give William nothing.

He avoided the subject as long as he could with Anna, then gave her a flat "No!" She had to give up. When he saw how deeply disappointed she was, he laughed ruefully.

"Lass, lass! Ye should 'a married the schoolmaister back in Wash."

Anna tossed her head. Schoolmaster indeed! Her sons were aiming beyond that. William was to be a minister; that was settled. Henry, the second son, wanted to study medicine. As for little Aleck, she planned to make him a lawyer.

Since her husband would not or could not help her, Anna turned to the Lord. "Ask and it shall be given unto you." Praying, she would fall asleep, to wake with the problem of William's schooling still unsolved.

One summer evening as she was resting in the dusk under her silver maple, William came and joined her. He told her he was fair discouraged. The precious years were slipping by; he was now eighteen and was getting nowhere.

Perhaps he and his mother had been mistaken, perhaps the Lord had not intended William should be a preacher. It might be His will that he learn a trade or succeed his father on the farm. Surely if the Lord wished him to preach, He would open the way for him to be prepared. A Presbyterian minister must be worthily prepared.

Anna said little, but William knew well enough how his words cut. When he had left her, she knelt down in the dark and prayed as she had never prayed before. Only a miracle could bring to pass this thing that she and William wanted. But it was a good thing — the service of the Lord — and she had a right to ask for it.

Unconsciously she raised her voice as she went on pouring her whole heart into her prayer. Not until she had breathed her fervent "Amen" did she notice a slight movement on the other side of the fence. Was someone there? Had she been overheard? No matter. There was no disgrace in praying in the garden, though she had always had a mind to keep her affairs to herself. She heard a horse's hoofbeats dying away down Sandy's road to Youngstown. But she went in to bed and thought no more of that until morning.

They were just sitting down to their early breakfast when a stranger in clerical dress alighted from his horse, knocked at the door, and asked to speak with Mrs. McGuffey alone. The Reverend Thomas E. Hughes may have been a pale, cadaverous, somber man, but when he explained that he was traveling to find pupils for his academy in Greersburg, Pennsylvania, that he had accidentally overheard her plea the night before, and would like to have her William — expenses could be arranged for — to Anna he looked like a bright angel from Heaven.

The upshot of it was that a week later William borrowed a horse, stuffed some clean socks and underwear and his few treasured books into a shabby saddlebag, and rode off beside the clergyman, undoubtedly the most hopeful lad in Ohio. He could have put the story into the *McGuffey Readers* as "The Mother's Prayer, or Piety Rewarded."

There are those who think that Anna McGuffey *knew*
the Reverend Mr. Hughes was passing by the fence when
she prayed so loudly in her garden. If so, she never admitted it.

Greersburg Academy, founded by the Presbyterian
Synod in 1802, was about thirty miles from the McGuffey home, on the thoroughfare from Cleveland to Pitts-
burgh. Promising lads from all over "New Connecticut"
and western Pennsylvania were welcome. The first sessions
had been held in a log cabin, with logs for benches, flat-
tened top and bottom by a whipsaw. But by the time
William arrived a square, substantial stone building had
been put up, and the place was known as the "Old Stone
Academy."

William must have been a likeable lad, for all his teachers seemed to have "adopted" him. Mr. Hughes had told
him there would be no tuition to pay. He might live in his
family and earn his board and keep by choring. The regular board of academy students cost seventy cents a week,
and the bill of fare at the dormitory never varied. Breakfast — coffee and bread with butter; dinner — bread and
meat and fruit "sauce"; supper — bread and milk.

In the principal's home William enjoyed slightly better
food and paid for it by hard manual labor. He shoveled
coal, carried wood and water, dug the garden, and fash-
ioned furniture for the pastor's wife.

Back at the homestead Anna smiled to herself as she
fingered William's latest letter in the bosom of her calico
gown and taught little Alexander his A B C's. The seventh
baby, a boy, they had named for his father, but they called

him Aleck. To Anna he was her ewe lamb, her "little Benjamin."

Aleck looked like his father, Sandy, slim and erect with clear blue eyes and thick brown hair. His four sisters petted him, and his father could never bear to whip him. They got him a pewter bowl and spoon — the other children had had only wooden ones — and he ate his mush and milk like a gentleman, gazing round the table with a withdrawn, fastidious air.

With this third son Anna had considered her family complete and was chagrined when a few years later she found there was another offspring on the way. Of course the Lord knew best. But it seemed to her there was a time for everything, and her time for childbearing was past. She was weary of the awkward pregnancies, of the sufferings of travail, of the care of infants, and the bother of them under her feet.

To cap the climax, the baby when it came was a girl, and they had quite run out of girls' names! Anna had used her mother's name and her own, that of her husband's sister Catherine, and of his sister Elizabeth, the poor girl who had died on the journey over the mountains.

So now let Sandy get out the big Bible and pick out any name he would. Sandy closed his eyes, opened the Holy Book, and put his forefinger on Genesis XLI:45. "And Pharaoh . . . gave him [Joseph] to wife Asenath the daughter of Poti-pherah priest of On. . . ."

Asenath it was, and Anna said if folks'd never heard that name, they'd not read their Bible from "kiver to kiver."

IX

WILLIAM COULD NOT SAVE any money at "Old Stone"; in fact, he never had a penny in his pockets. His father sometimes sent him a barrel of apples or a sack of meal for the principal, and his mother and sisters knitted him stockings and mittens and wristers and a long comforter for his neck. But clothes were a problem. However, it was no shame to be badly dressed at Greersburg; quite the contrary. Patches and darns were honorable, but not rags, holes, or unkempt hair. One was expected to be scrupulously neat in person, a good old Scotch-Presbyterian tradition. Still, the ministry looked a long way off.

The town fathers of a new school at Warren, Ohio were looking for a headmaster. William decided to apply. The salary would be small but regular. But he failed to qualify. At the oral examinations, two of the examiners, graduates of Yale, propounded questions he simply could not answer. Bitterly disappointed, he made a brave resolution. He would enroll at Washington College, near his father's old home in Pennsylvania, and get a thorough grounding before he attempted anything else.

He was twenty now; it might take him six years to get his degree, for he would have to work his way by school-teaching, at intervals, and by the hated farmwork. But the end would crown all. "Aim high," his mother told him, "second-bests aren't worth while."

Washington College was one of the many fledgling institutions of learning that had sprung up all over the West, poor in everything but hope and a small faculty of devoted men. Washington had opened as an academy in 1789, the year Billy McGuffey brought his family west. In 1806 it had been incorporated as a college and began to rival the older Jefferson College, located only seven miles away. (The two were logically united in 1865.)

The McGuffeys favored Washington because it had a Presbyterian tinge. During William's six years there, the president was a Scotch-Irishman — Andrew Wylie, barely thirty, a born teacher and a hard worker. Wick, Hughes, and Wylie, these three men were, after his mother, the moulders of William's career. Wylie, a patient, tolerant man with a fine sense of humor, taught classes all day and held conferences with his students in the evenings. He was their friend and counselor as well as instructor — the old-fashioned small-college president, more interested in the building of men than the raising of funds.

William's courses at Washington were Latin, Greek, Hebrew, ancient history, and philosophy. No modern languages, modern history, science, or mathematics. He never felt the lack. The subjects he took were those of the "higher education," the old scholastic curriculum that had been handed down from the days of Abélard and before.

Whatever William studied, he attacked with characteristic thoroughness and made completely his own. His prodigious memory was useful. For years he had known entire books of the Bible by heart. But it was impossible to memorize all the classics in four languages. So when he had no money to buy a needed book, he copied out the contents of a borrowed volume, word for word, and bound the pages by hand. Today at Washington and Jefferson they show a Hebrew grammar of William's, copied in this way.

In William's youthful career there were three turning points, the first when the Reverend Thomas Hughes providentially appeared at the farm, the second when he failed to get by the examiners from Yale. The third came when he was teaching school in a smokehouse near Paris, Kentucky, his junior year in college, and attracted the attention of a notable man, Robert Hamilton Bishop, of Edinburgh, who was scouting for professors for his new University of Miami in the little village of Oxford, Ohio.

Bishop was a Presbyterian minister, like all of William's good angels. He was also the most distinguished classical scholar in the West and an enterprising person. He had heard of William's attainments and his gift for teaching. He visited the primitive little school and watched the threadbare young teacher with the burning eyes and limber speech conduct his classes. He sought an interview and offered a professorship in ancient languages at Miami, salary $600.

William was dazzled. He would have to think it over. There was one "out" — President Bishop could not wait, the place must be filled at once. If William accepted, he would have to leave Washington without a degree. Would he ever be able to go back? And what about the ministry? He would have to consult his mother.

He arranged for a substitute to take over the Kentucky school and went back to northern Ohio, loaded as usual with his most valued possessions — his Livy, Virgil, Horace, the *Memorabilia,* and the Greek and Hebrew texts of the Bible.

He thought his mother looked ill and aged. But she greeted him as cheerfully as ever and, on the very first evening, turned over little Aleck's lessons to William while she sat by with sewing. But the lessons were not a success. Aleck was now ten years old, very wise and quite satisfied with himself.

While William was explaining a problem in arithmetic, lucidly but very lengthily, Aleck broke in, "Brother, never mind all *that.* What I want to know is, do you add, subtract, multiply, or divide?"

"Alex-and-er!" said William sternly, "that is not the way to *learn.* The object of learning is to *think. Think,* boy, *think!*"

Aleck, who had his mother's touchy temper, lifted his slate and banged it down on the kitchen table. Then, seeing that he had made a great crack across the precious possession, he burst into tears and flung out of the room.

Later in the evening, alone with his mother, William said, "If I go to Miami, let me take Aleck with me."

He was surprised when she agreed promptly. "Ay, son, that would be well done. He is fair spoilt among us all. You have a hand for children."

"I think I have," William acknowledged gravely. "And that brings me to what I have in mind." He told her about the conditions of the offer from Miami.

"What do you say, Mother? Dr. Wylie hinted there might be some place for me on the faculty at Washington if I stayed on. But it's Miami that draws me. They've nothing to do with, there in the backwoods — all's in the making. I've my own ideas about teaching, and I've a chance to pioneer. Can you understand my feeling?"

"Why not? To start things, to be the first on the ground, that is in our blood. Only *promise me*, William, that *sometime* you will be ordained, so that when the way opens, you may use your learning to preach God's word."

"Mother, I promise you that."

He kept his promise, but Anna did not live to hear him preach.

It was mild weather for January the morning that William and Alexander started south. All the family gathered at the gate, where the horses stood pawing the frozen ground. Impatiently Alexander mounted, while William deliberately tested the girths and attached the saddlebags. He looked self-conscious in the cheap new suit he had bought at the general store in Youngstown, his wavy hair slicked down over his ears with extra care.

"You should get you a new saddlebag, Professor," called his sister Annie pertly. "Yours are always bursted with your 'tarnal books!"

59

William's set face relaxed into a good-natured grin. But he deigned no reply. He intended his bags should be always bulging with books. Meticulously he removed his precious new spectacles and put them in his pocket — they had cost a pretty penny ordered from Philadelphia — wound his woolen scarf about his neck, mounted, and, removing his cap, stooped to kiss his mother.

"Good-by, my son." Anna kissed and blessed him.

Aleck reached his rosy cold face down to hers.

"Good-by, good-by, my Benjamin! God's blessing on you both!"

Now they were riding down McGuffey's Road, gone without a backward glance, their thoughts already with the future. For Anna their going was the beginning of the end.

Her son Henry was studying with a doctor in Pennsylvania and would soon be setting up in practice. Daughters were not the same. What use was it to give them learning? They married farmers, and that was the last of it.

Spring came, and summer, fall, and the long winter. Anna felt her strength slipping from her. She had always despised physical weakness, and she kept her condition sternly to herself.

William wrote to his mother every week. The trustees of Washington College had voted him his degree of A.B. without his having to complete his course there. Very gratifying. He had nothing to worry over now.

From little Aleck came every fortnight a prim, beautifully-written letter. He was a brilliant student, William told her.

How fast her sons were rising in the world. It fair frightened her. Sometimes the fear of death that lay at her heart like a stone gave way to another fear. Would worldly success and prosperity mislead her boys? William with his brain and his powers of speech, Aleck, who liked everything to be fine and grand — would they forget that such things mattered only if they were used for the greater glory of God?

Already she felt a separation of more than distance from these two, yet she would not have it otherwise. She had trained them up in the way they should go. In her practical way Anna decided that she must leave their future with themselves and God.

One day in the early spring of 1827, a letter was put into Anna's hands from William. He was being married — to a Miss Harriet Spining, daughter of Judge Isaac Spining, who held court in the log courthouse at Dayton, Ohio. As soon as he could manage it, William would bring his wife north for a visit.

For Anna another summer, fall, and winter dragged by. William wrote his wife had been poorly, he was taking her to Cincinnati to consult the noted Dr. Daniel Drake. After some months he reported Harriet's health improved. He was building her a brick house just off the campus, and when was his mother coming to visit them?

A brick house. What style! Suddenly Anna made up her mind to go *at once*. Sandy should drive her, and Lizzy, her fourth daughter, should go too.

Sandy selected a pair of horses, strong and steady, and put a mattress in the spring wagon for Anna's comfort.

Lizzy rode beside him on the box. On a beautiful spring morning they started bravely off.

At first Anna was in raptures and called out to the others in her old happy way. She noticed everything. How open the country was now, compared to the old hard days, how smooth the roads! She could gaze up at the sky when she lay back on her pillows; how beautiful the clouds, ever-changing, mysterious and far away! The earth was very beautiful, but she had always loved the sky most of all.

By noon her raptures faded. She was in great pain. The others, turning, saw her face distorted and tears raining down her cheeks. They could not quench her tears nor make her explain. She only pointed back along the road towards home.

Sandy headed the horses about, and by dusk they were back once more in the farmyard. Anna, still sobbing, was helped indoors and to bed. It was not the pain she cried with so long. It was the knowledge that she would never go to Oxford, never go anywhere again. Life, however difficult, had been so inexpressibly dear. How could she leave it and all those she loved, with her slow-blossoming hopes just coming into fullness? Yes, she believed in Heaven. But it was a strange place and very far away. And how lonely she would be there.

In a week she was back on her feet and took up her usual household duties as well as she could. No one saw her weep again.

She lived until the following January.

William and his wife had planned to come to her when the spring freshets were over and the mud dried in the roads. But suddenly the end drew near. Her three sons were summoned in haste. Henry, now a doctor, remained at her bedside day and night. And over the road they had taken so happily three years before, William and Alexander came galloping back. For them these years had flown. How long the time had seemed to their mother, little they knew.

When they came into her room she smiled at them, but she was already far away. The fearsome ordeal of death was over. The minister had been there to bring her "ghostly comfort"; she had acknowledged her unworthiness, professed her faith, and made her peace with God.

There had been heart-rending farewells, prayers said, and hymns sung by the family and friends kneeling beside the bed.

> O God, our help in ages past,
> Our hope for years to come . . .

But in her delirium it was not of religion nor of her husband and her children that Anna spoke. She was talking to her long-dead mother, and snatches of old ballads her mother used to sing came strangely from her lips. The tired old woman had become a little girl again, running barefoot in the clearing, chasing butterflies in the sun and fireflies in the dusk.

Anna's body was carried back to western Pennsylvania, to the old home that she had never revisited while she lived. The funeral was as fine as her wedding had been, long ago, and she was buried in the old Bedford Cemetery beside her own kith and kin, with space beside her for

Sandy when he should join her. Meanwhile he had a marble tombstone put up with an inscription that perhaps William wrote:

SACRED TO THE MEMORY OF ANNA,
WIFE OF ALEXANDER MCGUFFEY, WHO
DEPARTED THIS LIFE JANUARY 20TH,
1829. AGE 53 YEARS.

THROUGH THE WHOLE OF HER ADULT
LIFE SHE WALKED WITH GOD AND
HER DEATH WAS THE DEATH OF THE
RIGHTEOUS

There is no likeness of Anna Holmes McGuffey, nor any smallest scrap of writing from her hand. But her spark lives on through William's and Alexander's work. She had believed in the miracles of faith and work, but the success of the *Readers* would have sounded like a fairy tale to her. The McGuffeys never held with romance.

Miami University was seventeen years old when the
McGuffey brothers rode through the gates on an evening
in late January, 1826. Who but New Westerners would
have dared to call that modest cluster of three buildings,
fenced in from the main road of a crude village in the
woods, a *university?* True, the new president announced
that his faculty would offer a curriculum *as wide as any
in the United States.* The place seethed with plans and
aspirations — that was what made it so intriguing to William.

By this year of 1826, there were almost twenty times as
many people in Ohio as when William was born. And
still they came. As the old routes from the East were improved and the new ones opened, the human multitudes
increased in volume. Stages, wagons, canalboats arrived
packed and jammed. The newcomers spread all over the
frontier, reveling in the rich land and in the freedom of
thought and religion guaranteed by the great Ordinance

of 1787. They were an exuberant, noisy breed, united by a common ambition to be independent, happy, and prosperous — to get on in the world.

Something in the dizzy development of the West went to the settlers' heads. One Buckeye writer declared, "Without boasting, we aver and challenge the world to contradict the assertion, that this great and growing state possesses more of the essential ingredients of future greatness, and more self-sustaining and self-creating principles than any other territory of equal size on the face of the globe."

And down in Cincinnati, the thriving town that had grown up on the site of Sandy's old stamping ground, Fort Washington, the ebullient Dr. Daniel Drake made the rafters ring at a public meeting, proclaiming in a clarion voice that could be heard round the block, ". . . until the Ohio Valley was discovered . . . slow indeed had been the progress of society in the New World. . . . With the exception of the Revolution, little had been achieved and but little was in prospect!"

William McGuffey was not visionary and always kept both feet firmly on the ground. Yet he had his dreams. One of them was to become the most distinguished professor at Miami. The other was to bring some measure of culture to this teeming population, whose ignorance he had good reason to know from his roving schoolmaster days.

The third article of the Ordinance of 1787 had declared that "religion, morality, and knowledge being necessary to good government and the happiness of mankind, schools and means of education shall be forever encouraged." William vowed to himself that every Western child should have books and a free education. It was a wild dream for his day.

The brothers boarded with a professor's family, and ten-year-old Aleck took to academic society as a swan to a manor lake. He was to have an exceptional boyhood with many advantages and, though he and William never realized it, certain limitations. He was always with older and mostly very serious persons, and under his brother's supervision he became a prodigy of scholarship and deportment.

William held his nose closely to the grindstone and tried out all his pet theories on the bright boy. The teachings of Pestalozzi had reached America, and eager minds in the West caught them up.

William believed that a child should advance as fast as he could and would. Young Aleck learned Hebrew grammar before he did English and galloped along with his Latin and Greek because Brother William said the most difficult language should be mastered while the child's mind was fresh and pliant.

There was a sedate social life at Oxford, prayer meetings that had a sociable atmosphere and tea parties that were as solemn as prayer meetings. The president of the university was also the pastor of the Presbyterian Church.

Aleck went about with his brother, listened attentively to sermons and the conversation of adults, and managed his devotions and his manners with equal propriety. He had little time for physical exercise, and there were no organized sports at Miami. Indeed, William disapproved of competitive sports all his life. But young Aleck, if he wanted, could row on the river, or swim, play ball or marbles, or fly a kite.

The boy grew fast but remained slender. He never had the tough, sinewy physique of William, hardened by years of farmwork and tramping through the wilderness. Aleck was handsome, with his father's erect carriage, lordly head, and high coloring. He was and remained always a natural aristocrat, suave, reserved, and self-sufficient.

The country surrounding Oxford was of an enchanting beauty, especially in the spring, when the woods were filled with wild flowers, and in the fall, when the trees flamed red and gold. The wooded lanes, shady lawns, and cosy parlors were conducive to sentiment. At least so William thought. After his pinched youth he was beginning to expand in all directions.

And why should he not marry? He had a good salary. There was no earthly reason to wait. God knew how hard it had been for him to remain single so long. Most young men in the West married in their early twenties, and he was now twenty-seven. He bought himself the first of those black bombazine coats that later became famous. A certain country congregation considered him extravagant in dress, for bombazine was expensive stuff, but William knew it outwore all others in the end and went on wearing glossy black coats for the rest of his life. A white cambric clerical cravat instead of the fashionable black stock gave a touch of austerity to his appearance, but he had invested in a stovepipe hat and carried a handsome ebony cane.

Charley Spining from Dayton was a merchant in Oxford. That was the euphemistic way the Victorians had for saying a man kept a shop, for the old British prejudice against trade persisted in the new country. Only, instead of landed gentry, the Americans had a gentry of the learned professions. No matter if a man had come from the farm, if he had never worked behind a counter he looked down on those who did.

Charley's sister came to visit him, and William fell head over heels in love with her. Harriet Spining had a flower-like beauty, dark eyes velvety as pansies, a straight nose, a beautiful demure mouth, and glossy brown, natural curls hanging down her peachlike cheeks.

Harriet was gentle, conscientious, submissive. She had obeyed her parents and was prepared to obey her husband. From the first William planned their future, directed her reading, corrected her pronunciation. All with the kindest intentions, she knew, and she was grateful to him.

They were married on the third of April, 1827 at Judge Spining's farm, "Woodlawn," near Dayton.

The next year William built his brick house on the Miami campus. Stately French windows in front and a neat cornice round the roof lent dignity and elegance. "Anglo-Greek" architecture was all the rage. The McGuffeys began to live like gentlefolk. A village girl helped with the housework, and Harriet had time for embroidery and water-color painting.

William found his pleasure in starting a little school to try out some of his theories on primary education. The pupils were the children of his friends and later his own little girls, Mary and Henrietta, born in 1830 and '32. Mary was a roly-poly child, bursting with energy. She ought to have been a boy, William thought. But she made a splendid girl. Henrietta was a delicate, ladylike little creature.

The classroom was the yard behind his home where Harriet cultivated the inevitable flowerbeds, but where the logs lay just as they had fallen, cut from the primeval forest.

In this year began an educational project that was to influence American life profoundly for three quarters of a century. William divided the children into groups, one group to a log. Between times they were allowed to stretch their little legs running about in the open. The scheme was a great success.

The daily lessons William arranged for these classes gradually took shape as a book. The exercises and some of the stories were original, and other stories were selected and adapted from other books. He had already published in London *A Treatise on Methods of Reading*, which attracted some attention on this side of the water. By 1833 his *First Reader* was ready for printing, but it was several years later that he was approached by the Cincinnati publisher who was to make a fortune out of the *McGuffey Readers*.

In October of that year, 1833, William was ordained to the Presbyterian ministry. He wished his mother could have heard his first sermon. He preached regularly in the college chapel, and the attendance had never been so large. The students were required to come; but when William

Woodward College, 1831.

Cincinnati College, 1835.

William Holmes McGuffey in Civil War days.

Harriet Spining McGuffey.

Laura Howard McGuffey.

preached, the villagers came too. Soon he was in demand by congregations all over the state.

His sermons were clear, forceful, earnest, but never emotional. He had never undergone sudden conversion, nor urged it upon others, as his friend Lyman Beecher and the Evangelicals did. Souls were the strictly private concern of those to whom they belonged.

In belief he was a Fundamentalist, but in preaching he laid emphasis on character rather than dogma. He waked people up, made them think, never talked down to them nor over their heads. His figures were simple, his anecdotes homely and pungent, and he spoke in a natural conversational voice which was unusual in an age of Fourth-of-July oratory. He used no notes, so though he preached more than three thousand sermons in the course of his life, none of them survived in print. Prepared script hampered him.

Asked once how he could memorize a long sermon or lecture, William replied, "I do not memorize, it is not necessary, for if you have thoroughly thought out your subject, it is like a ball of wool you wind, leaving the end to come out of the center. You start to pull, and it simply unwinds naturally as you go along."

William's unwritten discourses are no loss, since his moral philosophy and metaphysics would interest no one now. What is worth knowing is that his pupils called his language "a well of English undefiled." In the first half of the nineteenth century there was nothing the people of the Middle West needed more than training in their mother tongue.

71

But it was *ideas,* not words, that interested William most. He had no intention of spending his life teaching the rules of dead languages, even though he could do it so well. Ideas were fluid, alive, and he wanted to dig deep down into the springs of human thought and behavior. He tried to exchange his courses in Greek and Latin for philosophy and religion, which were the courses President Bishop taught and, with his training at the great University of Edinburgh, taught well.

William persisted. At times the president and the young professor of classics hardly spoke as they passed each other on campus or in the halls.

After five years Bishop gave up the struggle and, in a reorganization of the faculty, turned over his courses to this upstart from the backwoods. William, in his dour way, was jubilant.

"Moral philosophy" went out of date forty years ago. But in Miami in 1830 William's course was the most exciting in college. Textbooks counted little, and a student who recited from them parrot-fashion would be promptly held up to scorn. Using the Socratic method, the professor promulgated, the students questioned, and the discussion wandered wherever their combined minds led. Though this was an age of academic stuffiness, no one was ever known to nod in McGuffey's classes.

By this time public schools were being opened all over the frontier, and in 1834 the first "College of Teachers" met in Cincinnati, not in fact a college but a national organization for meetings and discussions. William was an active member, constantly urging the need for better

72

training for teachers and for adequate school buildings. The publication of more and better schoolbooks was a project always close to his heart.

Not only teachers but leaders in other professions attended these meetings — Dr. Daniel Drake and his kinsman, Edward Mansfield, son of Colonel Jared Mansfield, Surveyor General of the Northwest Territory; Dr. Lyman Beecher, who had come to Cincinnati in '32; Calvin Stowe, who was to be sent abroad by the Teachers College to study the German school system; the scholarly Roman Catholic, Archbishop Purcell; Judge James Hall, editor of the *Western Monthly Magazine;* and James Handasyd Perkins, author of *Annals of the West.*

The town of Cincinnati had by now achieved its ambition to become "the Philadelphia of the West," and aspiring spirits from other parts of the country flocked to the new College of Teachers — Alexander Campbell, founder of the Disciples of Christ; Mrs. Lydia Sigourney, the Connecticut authoress; Thomas Grimké, that strange, saintly man from South Carolina who freed his slaves, advocated temperance, "fonetic spelling," and other odd causes, and "acted all his life as though things were *as they should be* and not *as they are.*"

All these aired their views and advanced their isms. Dr. Drake's ideas on education were considered wildly impractical. He advised the teaching of anatomy and physiology in the public schools and the enactment of a law *compelling* a man to give his children some kind of education! Even the New West, nursery of adventurous spirits, recoiled before such radicalism.

73

XI

GENTLE, DOMESTIC Harriet McGuffey would have been content to pass her life at idyllic Oxford. But fate ruled that she should be uprooted, torn from her pleasant home, and endure harsh unsettled years — fate, in the form of William's energetic patron and friend, Dr. Drake.

Daniel Drake's story is bound up with that of the McGuffeys. He was the son of a poor Kentucky farmer, an immigrant from New Jersey, who claimed descent from the great Sir Francis Drake and had vowed that at least one of his large brood should be made into a scholar and a gentleman. In 1800, the year William was born, the Kentuckian brought his young son Daniel, then fifteen, to Cincinnati to study medicine under an eccentric pioneer physician, Dr. William Goforth from New York City.

Cincinnati in 1800 had been a backwoods village of seven hundred people. Now, in 1828, the population was over 16,000. Drake had grown along with the town and had had a finger in every phase of its development. At forty-two he was not only the leading physician of the West, called in consultation all over the frontier, but an accomplished scientist, speaker, writer, and teacher. His ambition to make Cincinnati a leading medical center kept him forever embroiled in struggles with the smaller-minded doctors, who thwarted his grandiose schemes. Temperamentally Drake was torn between two inheritances: his mother came from gentle Quaker stock, his father from the fiery Saxon Drakes (or Dragons). With friends and family he was genial and gentle. In his fight for medical education he went forth breathing fire, prepared to use his tongue, his pen, and even his fists against all who opposed him.

He had married a niece of Colonel Jared Mansfield, a mathematician on the faculty at West Point Academy, whom President Jefferson had sent out to survey the Northwest Territory. She had been a brave and resolute woman, who accompanied her husband on his travels for medical consultation and research all over the West and South. Her early death of "autumnal fever" had been a tragedy from which Dr. Drake never recovered. For years he wore a mourning band on his sleeve and observed the anniversary of her death alone in his study, fasting and composing elegies to her memory. For in addition to all else, Daniel Drake found time to write poetry, a minor avocation in William McGuffey's opinion. Still, to compose acceptable verse was something he himself, with all the concentration in the world, could never do.

Drake was a tall man, spare and sprightly, with quick, gentle, nervous hands, eyes like an eagle's for keenness, with a curious dancing light behind them that illumined his whole expression. His nose jutted straight and strong as a cliff; his mouth was firm and sensitive; his golden-brown hair, touched with gray, waved back from a forehead high and serene. His ability, magnetism, and cocksureness made him the most respected, loved, and disliked man in Cincinnati. He had remained a widower, contrary to the custom of that day, when wives were promptly replaced, three, four, and five times. At his home, "Buckeye Hall," a center for the budding intelligentsia of the West, his mother-in-law presided and later his beautiful daughter Elizabeth, who from the first time he saw her attracted the fastidious eyes of young Aleck McGuffey.

The West was a small world in the 1830's and a hospitable one. Travelers from the East and from Europe included in their itinerary a voyage on the Mississippi and the Ohio, usually beginning at New Orleans and ending in Cincinnati. Timothy Flint, Charles Dickens, Mrs. Trollope, Harriet Martineau, the Basil Halls of Edinburgh, and a stream of others came to see what there was to be seen, were entertained, and went home to publish their impressions, usually unfavorable. Dickens liked Cincinnati, Mrs. Trollope hated it, Harriet Martineau doubted that she "had ever heard more sense and eloquence at any old-world tea-table" than at Dr. Drake's, Mrs. Basil Hall admired the scenery but felt the lack of liveried servants!

It was the custom for prominent citizens to call in person or to leave their cards at the hotel where a distinguished stranger was staying, with an invitation to midday dinner or high tea. Dr. Drake was famous for his breakfast parties. He would sally forth in the early morning and gather in any guests who sounded promising. The doctor's tastes and style of living were simple, his conversation sparkling. A baked apple with a cup of *good* coffee was his own favorite morning meal.

At his "Friday evenings" at "Buckeye Hall," guests of both sexes gathered to read original papers or indulge in "entertainment of a conversational character." Here one met the Beechers — the eloquent domineering Dr. Lyman; clever, talkative Catherine; quiet Harriet; learned, moody Prof. Stowe and his first wife Eliza Tyler, who sang charmingly. Also, General Edward King, father of Rufus, with his wife Sarah, daughter of the Virginian Thomas Worthington, second governor of Ohio; and always the highly "cultured" Hentzes, who ran a "fashionable" school for girls in Cincinnati.

Mr. Hentz was French; his wife, Caroline Lee Hentz of Massachusetts, was a fascinating bluestocking. She had won a $500 prize with her *De Lara, or the Moorish Bride, A Tragedy in Five Acts* and had published novels which were favorites in the West for two generations.

To mingle in such a galaxy, William McGuffey, and Harriet when she could leave her babies, eagerly traversed the thirty-six miles between backwoods Oxford and the metropolis.

We have a firsthand description of one of Dr. Drake's entertainments, a "pioneer party, for males only," in a letter from one of his guests.

. . . "When I arrived at Buckeye Hall, the two large parlors, which had been thrown together, were already filled. In the middle of one, on the center-table, stood a large stone jar in which was inserted a buckeye tree in leaf, which reached to the ceiling. The mouth of the jar was covered round the tree with moss. Ranged round the jar were small shells of pumpkins, filled with earth, in each of which was set a young buckeye branch, and the tops of the shells were set with the buckeye fruit and strewn over the table were limbs of the tree.

"In one corner of the same room there was a large stump of a buckeye tree which was used as a place from which to speak during the evening. In the other room, on a table, were two large buckeye bowls, one filled with popped corn, the other with apples; the former having many little round gourds to dip up the corn with. The company for some time amused themselves with the contents of the bowls, and with making acquaintance with fellow natives.

"After a while Ben and Charles Drake [brother and son of Dr. Drake] came in carrying between them a huge buckeye bowl of sangaree made from native wine, in which were floating several gourds. A bumper was then drunk to *Our Pioneer Fathers*, and other sentiments followed. . . . The sangaree promoted conversation and hilarity, so that all were quite agreeably employed, when the folding doors at the upper end of the room were thrown open, and a new scene greeted us: — a long table reaching across the room was covered with refreshments and vases of native flowers beautifully arranged.

"At one end of the table was a large urn of coffee, at which the elder Miss Drake presided [then not quite seventeen], and at the other end the younger Miss Drake [not yet fifteen], assisted by Mrs. Hentz, distributed spicewood tea. Both the coffee and the tea were sweetened with native maple sugar. On the table was cornbread, of various cooking, johnnycakes, pound cake made of corn meal, etc. Jerked venison was a favorite dish.

"After this we had some anecdotes from Dr. Drake, illustrative of the early history of the state, and one of a case where lynch law was applied for the stealing of a barrel of flour. Ben Drake contrasted the commerce and character of the country in 1816 with what it now is, giving us many valuable statistical facts which he had looked up with great labor and ingenuity. And we had a speech from the stump from Gen'l King. He addressed the married Buckeyes first in a few words, and then turning to the unmarried ones he told them to do as he had done, marry a Buckeye. . . ."

Dr. Drake collected gifted people, and he took the McGuffey brothers under his wing. When in 1836 he was reorganizing the Cincinnati College, he invited William to resign his professorship and become the president. It was an offer that promised well for the future; William left Miami, where he had been ten years, and moved to Cincinnati.

An earlier college in Cincinnati had closed in 1819 for lack of funds. Now Drake was resurrecting it on a grand scale, modeled after the German municipal universities, with departments of law, medicine, and liberal arts. Besides acting as president, William taught moral and intellectual philosophy; Edward Mansfield, constitutional law and history; Drake and two brilliant doctors from the East,

Samuel David Gross (great-grandfather of William C. Bullitt) and Willard Parker, medicine. This was the most imposing faculty ever assembled west of the Alleghenies. They should have succeeded, for they were all men in the prime of life, enthusiastic and harmonious.

But like many of Drake's innumerable projects the Cincinnati College failed for lack of money. The attendance was good and the public sympathetic, but not to the point of *financial* support. The panic of '37, the worst the country had known, was in full sway. With no endowment "except genius," no revenue but tuition fees, the college lasted exactly three years.

For William the connection, short as it was, had been valuable, widening his range and adding to his reputation. Daniel Drake, who was not then a member of any church, had seen to it that the charter should forbid the teaching of any sectarian theology, and under this provision William had definitely shaped his courses to exclude dogma. The series of Sunday-evening lectures on the Bible which he gave at Cincinnati College were immensely popular. The one on "The Book of Proverbs" jammed the chapel, and the "mechanics," who were not allowed in the auditorium, listened through a hole in the ceiling! These workmen who had built the hall enjoyed William's way of expounding the Scriptures as much as did the highbrows who squeezed them out.

Edward Mansfield in his *Personal Memoirs* wrote of William at this time, "He disentangled difficulties, made mysteries plain, and brought the abstruse and profound within reach of common intelligence. Dr. McGuffey was the only clear-minded metaphysician of whom it had been my lot to know anything."

When Cincinnati College closed in the summer of '39, William was promptly elected to the presidency of Ohio University at Athens, Ohio, and accepted. With what naïveté the pioneers selected names for their settlements — Oxford, Athens, Rome, Paris, Palmyra. Marietta, the first village in Ohio, had been named for Marie Antoinette.

Ohio University was the oldest in the state and had assured revenues, but in its thirty-five years' existence the registration had risen only from three to ninety. In the four years he served as president, William brought the attendance up to one hundred and ninety-six. But they were the unhappiest years of his life. He could never bear even to think, much less talk, of them all the rest of his life.

Their arrival in the new home began with domestic tragedy. In Oxford, two years after the birth of Henrietta, Harriet had presented William with his first son, named for himself. The baby had lived only three weeks. A year later a second son appeared, to comfort them. Harriet called him Charley for her brother; and a third boy, born the last year in Cincinnati, received the name of William's friend, Edward Mansfield. Soon after they reached Athens, the latest baby sickened and died.

Gone were the days of pure air, simple living, and few diseases. The pioneers had been able to give their children a better chance than these inhabitants of the new villages and towns who shut themselves indoors and coddled and dosed their offspring. Parents who lost only two or three of a brood counted themselves lucky.

Doctors had no idea of proper infant feeding. Nature pulled the strongest through; and if the physician helped, it was by using his common sense and insight, not by his bleedings and nostrums. Of Harriet's and William's three boys, only one, Charley, survived his babyhood.

The death of little Edward weighed down his father's spirits and made the crude village of Athens look a dreary place. The college grounds were bare and ugly, and he took it upon himself to set out some young elms (still flourishing today) and to have a fence built to protect them. To his utter astonishment these innovations were fiercely resented by the touchy villagers, who had always pastured their cows on the campus.

They stamped into the college and ordered him to take away that fence. He flatly refused, and from then on there was war. William received threatening letters and was jeered at and hissed in the streets. When he had to go into the remoter country for preaching or weddings, he armed himself with a horsewhip.

More serious troubles arose between the trustees and the farmers over the revaluation of the township lands on which the college relied for income. William got the brunt of the odium. One dreadful day he came home plastered with mud. He had been attacked in the street and mud-balls had been thrown. With a face like thunder he told Harriet to pack up — he was through.

With her velvet eyes brimming, but with a certain relief, Harriet obeyed her husband. Though where they were to go or what they should live on, she had not the least idea.

When weeks later they all drove for the last time through the gates of the offending fence, she noticed that one of little Charley's shoes was missing and turned to gaze anxiously at the road behind them.

"Don't look back!" commanded William sternly. "I never wish to set eyes upon that place again."

Charley began to whimper, and his father took him on his knees and diverted him with stories and pantomime all the long jolting way to Cincinnati. This was William all over. The uncompromising logician, the root-and-branch Calvinist, the sensitive Scottish temperament that never forgets and finds it difficult to forgive. Yet the same man who with little children could be patient, tender, and inspired.

XII

ALEXANDER WAS THE lucky one. Somehow in an age of wood and pewter he had managed to be born with a silver spoon in his mouth. Petted by his family, tutored by William, praised by the professors at Miami, he never knew the scrabbling struggles for a living and an education that his brother William had endured. Thanks to his Pestalozzian education, he graduated from Miami at sixteen and through William's friends secured a professorship of belles-lettres at Woodward College in Cincinnati. He took up his residence in that city and remained there a pillar of polite society for the whole of his long life.

Belles-lettres was that department of literature "in which taste and imagination are predominant." George Ticknor and Longfellow taught belles-lettres at Harvard. There were souls in the New West too who yearned to cultivate the beautiful for its own sake.

Aleck had taught himself French and Italian from books. He knew by heart selections from the *Elegant Extracts*, a set of six volumes of prose and verse published in England in 1808. At Miami he had pored over President Bishop's portfolio of fine engravings from Edinburgh. When he came to Cincinnati he took lessons from a German music master on the flute and clarinet. The Covenanters, like the Quakers, ignored the art of music. Even William considered Aleck's music lessons a waste of time. But he had to admire the picture Aleck made, slim and graceful, his heavy hair brushed back from his pensive brow, his blue eyes dreamy, as his long sensitive fingers moved along the stops of his flute, the notes sweet, smooth, brilliant, or shrill.

Woodward was not really a college. In their haste to create institutions of learning overnight, the Westerners tacked on these high-sounding names. Woodward was a high school modeled after the English public schools with the organization and title of a college. Unlike the English models, it offered tuition free. It was named for William Woodward, a far-seeing citizen of Cincinnati, who had donated a large tract of land and a sum of money for the purpose of "extending the rudiments of an English education to the poor children of the city and county for an unlimited period." The school had been in existence only a few years when Aleck took up his duties.

Naturally shy and fastidious, he found it trying to apply a veneer of culture to the illiterate and conglomerate mass of children who filled his classes. Well-to-do citizens were sending their children to private schools, of which there were several in Cincinnati by this time. Aleck labored conscientiously, but his heart was not in his work.

Mrs. Trollope's Bazaar, 1828–1829.

Fourth Street, west of Vine, in Cincinnati, 1835.

Alexander Hamilton McGuffey, about 1850, and
his oldest daughter, Anna. From a daguerreotype.

Cincinnati Landing, about 1835.

He gave up teaching and began to study law in the office of Benjamin Drake, a younger brother of the doctor. Lawyers in colonial days had not been highly regarded, but under the Republic the profession rose rapidly in public estimation and began to outrank the ministry.

Aleck with his shrewd, meticulous mind and imposing presence was to make a highly successful lawyer. But he had to gain most of his learning from books, as Ben Drake was a casual soul, more interested in dilettante literary pursuits and social life than in his law practice, and now remembered as a writer of short stories of the West.

Ben at this time was a debonair bachelor of thirty-eight and kept a journal, which is a continuous record of dinners, teas, and picnics by boat or horseback, tableaux-vivants, theater parties, concerts, dances, and cotillions. This in the era and environment that historians still describe as crude! The truth is, though their streets were muddy, houses unsanitary, servants unruly, and health indifferent, the members of the upper crust enjoyed themselves hugely in southern Ohio in the 1830's.

Ben Drake suffered from heart and lung trouble and had to be bled and cupped nightly by his brother, the doctor. But the journal passes lightly over such troubles to details of pleasant things. When Alexander McGuffey married the elder daughter of Dr. Drake on May 9, 1839, Uncle Ben Drake spent twenty-two dollars for a "very handsome breast-pin for the bride." Five hundred guests were bidden to the evening ceremony in "Buckeye Hall." And sixty or seventy friends called on the newlyweds daily in their new home on East Fourth Street.

Alexander's wife was tall and beautiful, with a style of her own. Her portrait done in the romantic manner by her father's protégé, Thomas Buchanan Read, makes her a queenly woman in a red-velvet laced gown, with oval face, fair and rosy; large, liquid hazel eyes; slim, arched nose; and crimson lips, rather firm than sweet.

Elizabeth like her father had a kind and generous nature. When, four years after her marriage, Brother William and his family were leaving Athens with nowhere to go, she urged Alexander to invite them to their home. They accepted, arrived bag and baggage, and stayed two years.

William was glum and depressed. The contrast between his present lot and Alexander's was trying. The older brother had slaved away his youth to make a bare living, and here he was in middle life stranded without a home, position, or prospects, while Alexander, at twenty-seven, seemed to have everything. As the son-in-law of Daniel Drake all doors were open to him. His practice grew rapidly, likewise his family, for Elizabeth presented him with a new baby each year. They kept four servants and had the best the markets and shops could supply. Alexander had none of the proverbial Scotch stinginess; on the contrary, he detested economies, as all good Westerners did.

The trustees of Ohio University had presented William with a set of complimentary resolutions to soothe his ruffled spirits and show that they at least appreciated him if the townspeople did not. But what he needed was money. His salary had been only fifteen hundred dollars, and he had saved very little. Alexander with the help of Dr. Drake came to the rescue and secured him a professorship in Woodward College which was more of a tribute to Woodward than to William, his friends thought. But everyone knew he would not have to stay there long. After his work on the effulgent faculty of Cincinnati College it was humiliating to come down to training high-school children. But William knew the value of early education. He did his best.

It was during William's two periods in Cincinnati, at Cincinnati College and at Woodward, that the famous *Readers*, the germ of which had long lain at the back of his mind, came to light.

Back in 1826 Winthrop B. Smith, a shrewd Yankee youth of eighteen, came out to Cincinnati from Stamford, Connecticut, determined to make his fortune in the West. He made it out of the *McGuffey Readers*, and a far larger one than he had ever dreamed.

For the first fourteen years he was in business, Smith was insolvent — but no one knew it. He had set up a small publishing establishment with a man named Truman on the second floor of a house on South Main Street. The Truman and Smith Company published and sold miscellaneous books, mostly reprints of standard works, which they thought would have a steady sale. Their first venture was a children's Bible, to which they added grammars, arithmetics, and primers. The returns were small indeed, and the firm was heading straight for bankruptcy when Smith put his sharp Yankee brain to work and evolved his Big Idea.

A great market for schoolbooks lay open in the West and South to the publisher who could manipulate it. The new country needed a new series of Readers suited to the demands of Western children and supplied near by. He cast about for an author to prepare such a set of books and approached Miss Catherine Beecher, who with her sister Harriet had established a school for girls in Cincinnati.

Catherine Beecher was one of the three great women pioneers for the education of their sex in America, but for some reason her fame has been eclipsed by the other two, Emma Willard and Mary Lyon. In her youth, Lyman Beecher's eldest daughter was engaged to Alexander Metcalf Fisher, "the mathematical genius of Yale," who had sailed away for a year's study in England and had been drowned in the wreck of the steamer *Albion* off the coast of Ireland. Catherine's fire-and-brimstone father refused to assure her that her beloved had gone to Heaven, since, though pious and upright, he had never undergone "conversion."

Poor Catherine's mental suffering ended in complete revolt against the old Calvinist dogmas, and that brought some relief. To salve her aching heart, she threw herself into good works and concentrated on the neglected education of women. By 1830 she was touring the West to raise funds for a girls' seminary.

She had published a book, *Suggestions on Education*, and she and her sister Harriet together had issued a small geography. Winthrop B. Smith thought Catherine might compile his school Readers. But she had never completely recovered from a nervous breakdown brought on by grief and overwork years before, and she preferred to devote all her strength to her crusade for female education. She knew, however, just the person to recommend in her place, her friend Professor William Holmes McGuffey.

Smith carried his proposal to William; William accepted and suggested his brother Alexander as collaborator. The series called for a Primer, a Speller, and four Readers. William had already planned a Primary Reader based on the lessons he had used in his informal classes at Oxford. He set to work on four others. The Speller he left entirely to Alexander, for whom the study of words had always had a fascination.

William's idea was to have the Readers lay the foundation of correct spelling, pronunciation, and usage. The texts should deal with subjects familiar to the children of immigrants and farmers and should exemplify American ideals of work, education, character.

Character — yes, the *moral* influence of these books William saw as most important of all. It would not be easy to make his pabulum acceptable to the conglomerate reading public of the West, a public made up of rationalistic Germans, devout and merry Irish, staid and pious Scots and English. But he *knew* he could do it.

He had lived with frontier people and shared their narrow, monotonous life. They needed to be cheered and entertained while they were being taught. To interest, to stimulate had always been the secret of his successful teaching. He would make the Readers interesting and suited to all tastes and all ages — often the parents would read and study with their children. He pictured the entire family gathered around a school Reader as they had gathered about the Bible, and the vision gave him a thrill of joy.

He would have no dogma, no mysticism, no dry sermonizing or gloomy or fantastic tales. Plenty of lively narrative about everyday country life, the blessings of industry, thrift, temperance, kindness, and patriotism. William believed very strongly in emphasizing the *practical* rewards of virtue — how like his mother's his religion was!

There should be stories about Indians — American children should know about the first inhabitants of their land. Old Sandy had often told his children the Indians were not so bad as they were painted. They were good, bad, and indifferent, like the white people, and according to their lights more often good than bad, if fairly treated.

The great Chief Logan had been as good as he was brave, "the friend of all men." And in the annals of the frontier there had been bad whites who were but little behind the bad Indians, in wiles, in cruelty and revenge.

The contract for the first series was signed by William on April 28, 1836. Truman and Smith were to pay him a royalty of ten per cent on all copies sold until the copyright should reach the sum of one thousand dollars, after which the Readers became the absolute property of the publishers. An extraordinarily clever bargain and one which Smith would never discuss in later years when the sales and profits had mounted to the millions.

The historic little books — a Primer, four Readers, and a Speller — appeared in 1837, attractively bound with green side covers and pictures on every page. Alluring pictures of children coasting, skating, boating, swimming, flying kites, playing ball. Earlier reading books had shown solemn pedagogues imparting instruction, philosophers and goddesses in togas and strange draperies. In the McGuffey illustrations children taught each other, talked with their parents, played with their pets.

The illustrated alphabet in the *First Reader* began with *A* for Ax. With what better symbol could a backwoods child begin to read and write? He had seen his father wield an ax ever since he could remember.

Many of the illustrations in the First Edition had been taken from English publications, and the costumes of boys and girls — the tippets, ruffled collars, and bowler hats — must have looked absurd to frontier children. But it was not William McGuffey's fault, nor Winthrop Smith's, that there were no artists in the West in 1837 who were able or would condescend to draw pictures for children's schoolbooks. In later editions illustrations were made especially for the *McGuffey Readers*.

The *First Reader* unlocked the gates of learning. The child learned with pleasure, reading of other children employed with familiar things. In the lessons, games were played for the joy of playing, life was lived for the joy of living, moral instruction was practical, never founded on the cruel judgment of a cruel God.

Animals played a prominent part. Of the sixty-three lessons in the *First Reader*, fifty have to do with horses, dogs, cats, birds, and smaller animate creatures.

The poetry, like the prose, was chosen not merely to edify but to delight. The *New England Primer* had groaned and warned:

In Adam's Fall
We sinnèd all. . . .

There is a dreadful fiery Hell . . .
Where wicked ones must always dwell.

McGuffey's First Reader exclaimed and sang:

The lark is up to meet the sun,
  The bee is on the wing;
The ant his la-bor has begun,
  The woods with mu-sic ring. . . .

.   .   .   .   .

See! oh see this shining thing!
It rests its golden glossy wing:
Its wing so bright with golden light;
Say, is it not a pretty sight?
  'Tis not a bird, 'Tis not a bee:
  Ah! it rises, up it goes;
  Now it settles on a rose.

Here was the ecstatic freshness of childhood presented to the children themselves in their own lesson-book. Life was meant to be enjoyed, not merely endured as a probation for the grave.

By some innate quality, a youthfulness of the heart that pierced and shone through all his Puritan severity, William divined how the young should be helped to learn. Both he and Alexander believed in the inalienable right of children to happiness.

The *Second Reader* led the child step by step into the enchanted garden.

The *Third* contained unforgettable stories, "Harry and the Guide Post," "George Washington and His Little Hatchet," and the "Seven Sticks" (in union is strength). Also poetry, fables, dialogues, and the Lord's Prayer in verse.

In the *Fourth Reader* one began to get the real McGuffey classics — "Casabianca," "The Old Oaken Bucket," "The Arab and His Horse" — and first lessons in natural history and physics. Many of the frontier children left school when they had mastered the *Fourth Reader*. At that, they received much in little.

Although the first series of Readers was so satisfactory, in 1841, four years after their publication, Messrs. Truman and Smith were not prospering. To succeed in the widely scattered Western market salesmanship was needed. Smith was his own best agent, and Truman no help whatever in that line. The time had come to separate, so the astute Smith announced, and the less perceptive Truman was willing.

On the day set for their dissolution of partnership, Smith arrived first at their dingy little shop and proceeded to assemble all the sample books on a table, in two heaped-up lots. In one he placed the firm's miscellaneous publications, *The Child's Bible with Plates by a Lady of Cincinnati*, *Mason's Sacred Harp*, etc., etc., — a rather dreary lot, but on top of the volume he piled most temptingly all the cash the firm possessed!

In the second lot he placed six small textbooks, including the four *McGuffey Readers* and the *Speller*. (The *Primer* seems to have faded away, as superfluous in the series.)

When Mr. Truman arrived, Smith exhibited the two lots and gave him his choice. Truman promptly gathered up the larger stack of books, plus the cash, and departed well-satisfied. One hears of him no more. Winthrop B. Smith had made himself sole owner of the *McGuffey Readers*.

His first act was to extend the series. Alexander's Speller, though very successful, had been overshadowed by William's Readers. Now, however, Smith entrusted the younger brother with a task which was to crown all, the preparation of an advanced Reader, to initiate frontier children into the beauties of literature and the arts of elocution and oratory.

Alexander, as a professor of belles-lettres, was known for his cultivated taste. Smith gave him *carte blanche*, and William, always more interested in abstract ideas and original theories of education, took no part in the work. It was the youngster's own field, and he could do it well. Alexander's was not an original mind; it was accumulative, selective. He browsed over the whole field of English and American literature and brought forth an anthology remarkable for the time and place, *The Rhetorical Guide*, a book of "Elegant Extracts in Prose and Poetry."

Alexander thought Americans, especially Westerners, were not awake to the fact that they had a national literature. He would show them. To selections from the English classics he added others from the works of Cooper, Irving, Bryant, Fitz-Greene Halleck, and Lydia Sigourney, and from the writings of his own and his brother's friends and kinsmen, Thomas Grimké, Lyman Beecher, Edward

Mansfield, and Daniel Drake. The *Fifth* and *Sixth Readers*, into which Alexander's *Rhetorical Guide* was later expanded, were to mould the tastes of four generations. For many a household they were, with the Bible, the sole source of mental enlightenment, for many a self-educated man his only Alma Mater.

Besides introducing the older boys and girls to literature, Alexander's *Guide* trained them in public speaking and reading. William had advocated reading aloud as the backbone of elementary schooling. Alexander wished to perfect the process to an art. He urged Americans to have "music masters of the reading voice," as the ancients had. They should devote years to this accomplishment, with the same devotion they would give to becoming an accomplished performer on a musical instrument.

His idea appealed to the West. Republicanism and oratory were strongly associated in the Western mind. For generations future congressmen were to get their first training spouting Alexander's selections on the school platform on "Exhibition Day."

> Sink or swim, live or die,
> Survive or perish,
> I give my *hand*, — and my *heart*, —
> To this vote!

> . . . . .

> I know not what course *others* may take; but
> as for me, give me *liberty*, or give me *death*. . . .

If William was a missionary laboring to correct the wretched frontier vernacular (prefacing elementary Readers with admonitions to

97

"Utter each word distinctly. Do not say *Ole* for *Old*, *Heerd* for *Heard*, *Turrible* for *Terrible*, *Narrer* for *Narrow*, *Canady* for *Canada*, *Muskit* for *Musket*, *Cus* for *Curse*, *At* for *Hat*, *Busts* for *Bursts* . . ."),

Alexander was the apostle who preached the beautiful art of reading and speaking. A large amount of space in the *Fifth* and *Sixth Readers* was given over to exercises in "Articulation," "Inflection," "Accent and Emphasis," "Reading Verse," "The Voice and Gesture."

The *Rhetorical Guide* appeared in 1844, and for his epochal work Alexander received a lump sum — five hundred dollars and no royalties. To the young lawyer, for literary work done on the side, this amount probably seemed not only sufficient but munificent. No doubt Smith knew where the munificence really lay.

He himself worked like a beaver, getting the *McGuffey Readers* introduced into schools all over the West, South, and East, everywhere but in New England, where the "Worcesters" continued to be used. At first Smith was his own agent; later he initiated a trusted assistant, another Yankee, Obed Jay Wilson of Bingham, Maine. Wilson had been a schoolmaster and knew more about the inside of a book than Smith ever did. With his book knowledge went a keen flair for business. Soon Wilson had a large corps of agents under him, scouring the country, visiting schoolboards, buttonholing legislators. Smith in Cincinnati looked after the publishing end. In 1852 he took his wife's two brothers, Edward and Daniel Sargent, into the firm. His own brother managed an affiliated firm in New York.

98

Before 1860 the location of Cincinnati on the Ohio River with facilities for cheap transportation had enabled Winthrop Smith to get control of the schoolbook trade of the entire South. There were at that time no schoolbooks published in the Southern states, and the "McGuffeys" went like wildfire. The Civil War put an end to all the distribution, and Smith's firm suffered correspondingly. But luckily for them the Methodist Book Concern in Nashville, Tennessee undertook to reprint the "McGuffeys" for the Confederate children, and this action held the market for the Cincinnati publishers. As soon as any part of the South was strongly occupied by the Federal forces, orders would come in to Cincinnati for fresh supplies from the firm there. Thus their trade was unexpectedly held for them.

Fluctuations in the price of materials during the war, due to the use of paper money, worried Winthrop B. Smith, and his health began to fail. In '63 he decided to retire from active business, but he remained as "special partner" and continued to grow richer year by year, as did his brothers-in-law Edward and Daniel Sargent and the ex-schoolteacher from Maine, Obed J. Wilson. In fact, the Midas touch seemed to descend upon all connected with the booming concern.

As time passed, other partners were cautiously admitted. Anthony H. Hinkle, a skilled binder and manufacturer; Caleb Bragg of Cleveland, a bookseller; Lewis Van Antwerp, accountant; and, still later, two trusted employees — Henry H. Vail and Robert F. Leaman. The firm changed from W. B. Smith and Co. to Sargent, Wilson and Hinkle;

later to Van Antwerp, Bragg and Co., called by their rivals, who were many, "Van Ante-up, Grabb and Co." Other sobriquets sourly bestowed, in a day when the words sounded novel, were "Monopoly" and "Octopus."

The wars of the Readers were long and bitter, especially the famous one between the "McGuffeys" and the "Appletons." The "McGuffeys" always won. Edition followed edition, revised and brought up to date from time to time, but still bearing the strongly distinctive imprint of the original authors.

The total sales are estimated to have been one hundred and twenty-two million.

Tradition says that at Christmas time a certain member of the publishing firm used to have a barrel of choice hams shipped from his Cincinnati packing house to Professor McGuffey in Charlottesville. And that William's second wife received shawls and breastpins from a similar source.

William accepted these sops politely but absent-mindedly. Absorbed in his world of books and thoughts, he gave little attention to money or material things.

But people persisted in asking why he had sold his copyright for a mess of pottage, and he finally grew quite touchy on the subject. He would reply "that the time, labor, worry, expense of the introduction and distribution of the books fell altogether on the publishers, and they were entitled to *all* the pecuniary profits. . . ."

No member of the firm ever offered the haughty Alexander hams or breastpins. If they had, he would probably have returned them with the frigid intimation that he could supply his own needs.

When in later editions the publishers, for business reasons, printed Alexander's name on the title pages of the *Fifth* and *Sixth* in small type, hoping the public would not notice the initials of the author were A. H., instead of the better-known W. H. McGuffey, Alexander asked to have his name left out *altogether*. This was done, and so he became the forgotten man of the story.

Three elements went into the success of the *McGuffey Readers:* first, the intellectual hunger of the New West; second, the vision of the two gifted men who understood that need; and third, the salesmanship that brought the goods to the market.

But more difficult to analyze, for those who were not brought up on "McGuffeys," is the mysterious hold the books have upon those who were. They did something to one. And not only to the illiterate pioneer children whose minds had nothing else to feed on. The *Readers* were widely used down to 1900, and in some localities later, and their devotees today are men and women who were brought up in the prosperous decades between 1890 and 1910, and often in bookish homes.

Let their eyes light upon a reprint of a McGuffey illustration, and their faces will relax into a happy smile. Put one of the old books into their hands, and their fingers will close affectionately over it. Turning the leaves, some spring loosens in the frozen heart's core and a thousand memories, painful and sweet, rush into the mind. Faces of teachers, of boys and girls, long forgotten, rising out of the misty past, again to be loved, feared, and hated. Tramps through snow and rain and heat with a satchel of books and a tin lunchbox. Passionate friendships, quarrels, confidences, kisses. Long hot afternoons given over to "McGuffeys" while orioles call beyond the open windows and the fragrance of lilac and syringa floats tantalizingly by.

True, the children were drilled so long over these "pieces" that all grandeur and pathos faded out. But who can ever forget them? The first thrill comes back now as they are read over again after all these years. They are a part of the very stuff of one's mind forever.

Tastes were neither pampered nor stinted. Madness, torture, and death were considered suitable subjects for older children, if expressed with force or beauty. So they had "The Maniac," "The Crazy Engineer," "Conflagration of an Amphitheatre," and the horrific scene between Hubert and little Prince Arthur in "King John." But they were luckier than the modern child. The reading of the horrors stimulated the imagination but left it free to work. The child who sits before a moving picture has all his imagining done for him.

XIII

William McGuffey once observed, "Some men are helped by a discipline of adversity; some by a discipline of prosperity. As for me, I always was best under a discipline of prosperity."

In his drudging youth he had been solemn and repressed. As a budding professor at Miami, he had expanded happily. Now again, at Woodward, holding an uncongenial job and living partly on his brother's bounty, he was neither happy nor inspired. The year 1845 found him dutifully pegging away, longing for better days, when suddenly two good openings offered at once.

His latter-day angel, Daniel Drake, who had influential friends on the faculty of the University of Virginia (he had declined a professorship there himself in 1830), sent in William's name for a vacancy in the chair of moral philosophy. William heard rumors of this but could hardly take them seriously. Nothing could have been more flattering than an offer from the famous institution. But he believed only Episcopalians and infidels were acceptable in that stronghold of aristocrats and freethinkers, and he was a dyed-in-the-wool Presbyterian. What would they want of him?

The official invitation came along in due time, and a second offer immediately after. William was asked to become pastor of the prosperous First Presbyterian Church in Dayton, Ohio; and, tempted by the fact that he and Harriet had warm friends in her old home town, he hesitated, half-inclined to throw over Virginia. After all, the South was a far and strange part of the world to them both.

But he reckoned without his sponsor. Dr. Drake saw things in the large. He wrote William one of his impetuous letters: "Your going to Dayton is *out of the question*, not indeed to be thought of *for a moment*." And to clinch the matter, he enclosed a check for fifty dollars and practically *ordered* William to proceed to Charlottesville at once.

William McGuffey was a strong-willed man. But Daniel Drake was older, more celebrated, and equally determined. To resist him would have meant a struggle. William accepted the fifty dollars as a loan, went to Virginia, and remained for the rest of his life.

The University of Virginia was still young when William arrived in '45. Incorporated in 1804, it had opened its doors in 1819, the same year Ohio University was founded. But what an air of finish and beauty it had, compared to the crude Western colleges William had known! Unkempt villages and college administration at sixes and sevens had been the background against which he had struggled to do his intellectual work. Here he found velvet turf, ancient trees, and classical buildings. Thanks to the taste and genius of Jefferson, the college had already an air of mellowness and repose, an ideal atmosphere for William's scholarly and somewhat weary spirit.

He had always thought of Thomas Jefferson as a statesman of wild and subversive tendencies. But he had to acknowledge the Virginian knew how to build a home for learning. The buildings, halls, dormitories, and faculty homes of mellow brick lined a long rectangle, headed by an administration building, The Rotunda, modeled after the Roman Pantheon. A professor's house with adjacent dormitories under his supervision was called a "Pavilion." William's was No. 9, a square, two-storied neo-classical house with French windows and one of those many pillared porticoes that Jefferson loved.

William's daughters had been left in Ohio to finish their year at the famous boarding school of a Dr. Beattie in Steubenville. Mary was sixteen, plump, jolly, and clever; Henrietta, fourteen, a docile die-away Victorian miss. When they came South their father allowed them to make the trip unaccompanied, over the newly-opened Baltimore and Ohio Railroad, high adventure in 1846. The train lurched and swayed through the mountains, and both girls were violently car-sick.

At Baltimore they spent the night with relatives, who served oyster stew for supper as a special treat for the Westerners. The girls had never seen an oyster in their lives, but they swallowed their portions politely, though

Mary said afterwards that when she got the first oyster down she felt as though she had swallowed a baby. Until 1850 she and Henrietta never tasted an orange, a lemon, or macaroni.

At Charlottesville, William thawed and flourished. He smiled more easily, lost some of his moodiness, and enjoyed life as it came. His classes were as always very popular, and he was soon lecturing and preaching all over Virginia. His conservative theology was generally approved, and he was liked for his force and fire and the honest simplicity that was all his own.

One uphill task, at which he worked incessantly, as he had in Ohio, was the establishment of free schools. State schools did not appeal to the class-conscious Virginians. Governor Berkeley, in 1671 fervently thanking God there were no free schools in Virginia, had spoken for his class. The planters always preferred to educate their children under private tutors. For the others nothing was planned. Until 1700 probably less than half the people in Virginia were able to sign their names.

Thomas Jefferson had tried to work out a free compulsory system of education for his state without success. And even in 1845 Virginia was not yet ready for William McGuffey's earnest proposals. He worked for this cause for twenty years. But it needed a terrible civil war to make Virginia accept a public-school system, forced upon her as a condition of her readmission to the Union.

Harriet McGuffey found Southern housekeeping difficult. She could not cope with the colored servants' trifling ways. As she and William would not own slaves, they had to rent them and were expected to send them back to their owners for punishment when they misbehaved. Since this meant whipping, the McGuffeys preferred to rely on moral suasion. Generally the results were far from satisfactory.

Their sixteen-year-old daughter Mary said the Southern system was all wrong. How could people be *whipped* into a moral sense? She would show what *she* could do. The McGuffey's butler, a bright young colored man about her own age, named William Given, was eager to learn to read and write, and Mary began to teach him.

"You can't do that," her father remonstrated, "it's against the law of Virginia."

"Don't care if it is," retorted the chip off the old block, "I am going to do it anyway." And she did.

William Given more than fulfilled her hopes. After the Civil War he entered one of the newly-opened schools for Negroes and studied for the ministry. Mary McGuffey used to go to hear him preach whenever she was in Washington, D.C., where he was pastor of the first Colored Presbyterian Church. He married an ex-slave named Isabella, whom he had taught to read, and who became a schoolteacher in Charlottesville.

Isabella was ahead of her time. She continued to hold her job after marriage and brought up her children in Virginia, where William joined them when he could spare time from his work in Washington. He never failed to call at the home of Professor McGuffey, bearing gifts of fruit, game, and "beautiful Potomac shad."

Long, hot Southern summers, Negro servants, and a plague of ants wore down William's transplanted wife.

The low-built, shaded campus houses were damp and infested with a species of ant, very small, very red, and very active. They swarmed in the sugar barrel, marched over the fresh-baked bread and cake, floundered in the molasses jug, and drowned in the coffee cups. Harriet battled them by day and in her dreams at night.

One day she entered her husband's study only to flee precipitately before his wrath. He was standing by the open window casting out red ants with a fine-tooth comb as he extricated them from his sparse red hair.

Five years after the move to Virginia, Harriet went back to her old home in Dayton to spend the summer and was taken desperately ill with inflammation of the bowels, as appendicitis was then called. Patients were treated with applications of hot compresses, suffered agonies, sometimes recovered, more often died.

Harriet died before William could reach her. He arrived at the old farmhouse where they had been married, to find her already laid out in her coffin. Looking down at her dead face, untouched by the brief illness and young and lovely in its waxy stillness, he was overcome with grief and regret. His wife's sweetness, her sufferings, the cares he had brought upon her, all rose up to smite him. Religion and philosophy, all the stern resolution of centuries of Scotch Puritanism seemed to fail him in that hour. He could not be reconciled.

He went back to Virginia and buried himself in his books. But he was lonely and all at sea. He resolved to try a change of scene and in the summer of 1851 set out with his daughters and his only son, Charley, now 15, for a tour of Ohio, the White Mountains, and the St. Lawrence country.

The McGuffeys and the Drakes were great travelers. Dr. Drake traveled for medical research, William and Alexander for pleasure, whenever they could. In the '40's and '50's these people had still the restlessness of the pioneers and gladly left their comfortable homes to endure the discomforts of the new railroads and the old river steamers, risking the perils of fevers or the mysterious plague of cholera that lay in wait in strange places.

Cholera was supposed to have been brought from India to England. In 1832 it broke out in Quebec on an emigrant ship from Ireland, traveled west on the St. Lawrence steamers, swept over the Great Lakes, down the Mississippi, and up the Ohio to Cincinnati. Summer after summer it reappeared and ravaged the Middle West. In the worst of all epidemics, that of 1849, Alexander and Elizabeth lost a six-year-old daughter. All their lives the other children remembered that terrible time. They were lifted up in their father's arms to kiss their sister's chilly lips where she lay in her little white coffin, their mother, dry-eyed and stony, looking on.

"Look well," she said, "so you will always remember Etta."

It was a time beyond tears.

By July of that year there was scarcely a family in Cincinnati that had not lost at least one member. There was no panic, but the city lay under a malignant spell. Coffins and medicines were at a premium. Bells tolled, and special prayers were offered in churches.

Dr. Drake promulgated preventive instructions. Great coal fires were kept burning in the streets day and night "to purify the air."

The mistaken treatment of the sick and dying was cruel. The victims cried in their agony for water, water, and it was always refused. All the medical men agreed that no water should be given. But none of them knew how the disease originated nor how it was transmitted.

Dr. Drake advanced a theory of his own. He believed the disease might be carried by "animalculae, so minute as to be undetected, but capable of subsisting on persons, or pursuing an independent track in the atmosphere. . . ." But his brilliant anticipation of the germ theory had, at the moment, only slight practical effect.

He advised the city fathers to clear up the refuse in all streets, gutters, yards, and slaughterhouses, to drain all stagnant water and sprinkle chloride of lime about. This they did. But the popular belief that cholera was caused by "an aerial poison, a miasm or malaria, which floated in the air," especially the night air, persisted; consequently it was considered most important to keep the windows in the bedrooms of both sick and well tightly closed.

Two years after the great epidemic of '49 William McGuffey dared to bring his children into the cholera belt at the most dangerous season. But since nobody really knew how or why the disease originated, nobody changed his plans because of it. William came North for consolation and diversion. What he ran into was stark tragedy.

In Cincinnati the travelers were the guests of Alexander; and in Dayton, of the Spining relatives. As usual

William Holmes McGuffey, about 1860. The
likeness preferred by his family.

Bird's-eye view of Cincinnati and its surrounding hills.

Pavilion No. 9, University of Virginia, the home of William Holmes McGuffey.

The University of Virginia, as planned by Thomas Jefferson.

there were rumors of cholera about, but the cases were said to be few. The party spent a night at Niagara and went on to Burlington, Vermont, arriving on a fine Sunday evening. After supper at the hotel, they all walked out to see the sunset on Lake Champlain. As "the great red bubble" sank below the water's rim, young Charley exclaimed with a sigh, deep-drawn and wistful — his sister Mary remembered afterwards — "Well, it's gone!"

At midnight the lad was stricken with a violent attack of cholera and died before morning. This time William's despair was beyond revolt. He accepted his fate. His shoulders drooped, his ravaged face settled into furrows, and his eyes assumed a sadness that they never lost.

Somehow he managed the nightmare journey with poor Charley's body back to Dayton for the funeral. Somehow he found himself again at his desk in Charlottesville. But he was unfit for work, unfit for anything.

In September, a year and two months after Harriet's death, he found comfort in the willing arms of Miss Laura Howard, daughter of the dean of the university.

It was considered by the faculty a suitable match for a widower of fifty-one. The bride was neither too young nor too old, her background was sedately academic and Presbyterian. Also, she was a Southerner and "knew how to keep Negro servants in their place."

She never interfered when William went out of his way to show kindness to a colored person, as he often did. Though no abolitionist, he had a special sympathy for the race; and when he preached, the Negroes' section of the church was always crowded. But the new wife drew the line at receiving her stepdaughter's protégé, William Given, in her parlor. When he arrived she withdrew to an upper room.

Aside from this subject Laura and her husband were as one. The domestic difficulties that had persisted under the Northern wife were things of the past. Red ants never got out of hand in Laura's house. She kept little dishes of ant poison under the legs of every table, chair, and bed.

She was a tall woman with rather sallow skin, dark hair, fine dark eyes, high cheekbones, a long upper lip, and a prim but kindly mouth. In later years she relieved her plainness with long slinky curls that half-covered her sunken cheeks. Of course she longed to give William a son, but instead she produced a daughter, called Anna for William's mother. The child lived to be only four years old, and Laura never tried again.

Her stepdaughters married, Mary a Dayton physician and Henrietta a Miami professor, serious men after William's heart and of the same Scotch-Irish breed. After his girls had moved back to Ohio William was left alone with his new wife in the Cranford-like tranquillity of a Southern college community before the Civil War. He could not feel the loss of his last child as Laura did. It had been her first, and she knew it would be her last. But the waves of sorrow had broken over William's head too often, and he was inured to domestic grief. It was the current of national unrest that troubled his spirit now. He was a Northern anti-slavery man settled permanently in a Southern community, married to a Southern woman. How should he ever ride out the coming storm?

XIV

WILLIAM'S PATRON, Dr. Drake, died in '52; and his father, old Sandy, in '55. After the death of his aspiring Anna, Sandy had married "an estimable lady," so illiterate that she could not sign her name. She kept his house and bore him three daughters and took care of very old Billy and Ann, the immigrants, until they died, William at ninety-four, Ann at ninety.

They all moved back from northern Ohio to western Pennsylvania. There, among the scenes of his exciting youth, Sandy's life ran out in a peaceful pattern. Sitting for hours in the sun, his grandchildren swarming about him, he had time to think over the changeful years.

How differently his and Duncan McArthur's lives had shaped. Duncan had studied surveying, got rich speculating in land, served in the War of '12, was made a general, then governor of Ohio, and had lived in luxury at his elegant estate "Fruit Hill" near Chillicothe. At the end Duncan's luck had turned. He'd been crippled by the fall of a rotten porch roof, shut up in his room for years before his death back in '39. A rum mischance after all his hair-breadth 'scapes from Indians, Britishers, and political cranks.

He, Sandy, had stayed at farming. Yet — and this was strange — he wouldn't change his lot for Duncan's or Dr. Drake's or anybody's. He would leave behind him little money and a name distinguished only for honesty and industry. But his three sons had risen by their brains higher than their wishful mother had ever dreamed.

William, the professor, was at the top; Aleck, the lawyer, was climbing fast. Henry, the third son, was a country doctor in "Kaintuck," a kindly modest man, loved by his patients, and the best talker in the family. A poor collector though; money was the last thing Dr. Henry McGuffey cared about. Like all the rest of the tribe!

For himself, Sandy was thankful to have kept his health and his independence. And to be able still to enjoy each day as it slipped by, one like enough to another. Yet all different, too, in this chancy climate, what with sun and rain, thunder and lightning, frost and snow, and spring always a-coming 'round again! With the crops and the beasts and the floods to mind, time never hung heavy on a farmer's hands, even if he had to let other folks do most of the work, as Sandy had to now.

For what went on in the cities he cared less, though he was proud of his country, proud to have lived as one of the first settlers in the great Northwest Territory, and afterwards through the greatest Period of Progress in History — that was what the newspapers called it.

Sandy told himself he had had a full, rich life. "The earth is the Lord's and the fullness thereof. . . ."

Sandy the Scout was eighty-eight when he died and was buried beside Anna, the love of his youth.

Something of him must have gone into the *McGuffey Readers*. He loved the outdoor life and all living things, was simple, sensible, brave, and peace-loving, a true American.

His life spanned the best period of American history, the years of ferment and fervor between the Revolution and the Civil War. The nation was seething and chafing, shaking off the influence of Europe, fighting orthodoxy, intemperance, slavery, illiteracy, beginning to enjoy books, nature, and to be conscious of its own identity.

Sandy's sons had begun their lives and accomplished their most lasting work in this era. But William's life lapped over into the disillusioned Reconstruction years; Alexander lived on into the flimsy Gilded Age.

In politics William and Alexander had been Whigs. The Whig party under Henry Clay, friend and idol of both Drakes and McGuffeys, had at first ignored or evaded the slavery issue, then finally declared it settled by the great Compromise of 1850. The policy had appealed to the McGuffey brothers, who, much as they disapproved of slavery and the extension of slavery, were terribly afraid of radicalism and violence.

But violence it was to be. Neither compromise nor negotiation, nor gradual and peaceful emancipation, of which many moderates talked, could dispose of the burning question. It was to be settled only after four heartbreaking years of bloodshed and fanatical contention. The McGuffeys were too old to fight, but their mental sufferings were undoubtedly intense. Bad enough for Alexander in Cincinnati, just over the border from Kentucky, but infinitely more trying for William, teaching in a stronghold of States Rights doctrine. There was just one thing to do, and he did it. He held his tongue.

The old friends and leaders — Drake, Clay, Webster — were dead, and he sometimes envied them their escape from the dilemma in which he found himself, from the disillusionment of seeing all they had worked for fail.

Through the Dred Scott decision, John Brown's raid, the election of Abraham Lincoln, Secession, Virginia's decision to join the Confederacy — tight-lipped and grim, William lived on at Pavilion No. 9.

His students left him to enlist; his classes dwindled away; Laura worked for the Confederate soldiers; he ceased to hear from his brother and daughters in Ohio, all ardent for the Union cause. He grew old and sad and increasingly taciturn. Inwardly he deplored Secession and wished for the victory of the North. But he loved his wife's people, his students were like sons to him, their sufferings his, and his heart bled for them.

Often he thought of his lost son Charley, who would have been sure to enlist, had he lived. On which side? The Union, of course.

When the war ended, the publishers of the *McGuffey Readers* bestirred themselves promptly to find out how peace was going to affect their sales. They invited William to tour the South at their expense and bring them a report on conditions. He was sixty-six when he agreed to undertake this strenuous trip through Georgia, Alabama, Mississippi, and the Carolinas. In all the larger towns he was entertained as an honored guest at the home of some graduate of the University of Virginia.

What he observed was tragedy. This was the era of "carpetbaggers" and "scalawags," of the Ku Klux Klan, of the South's deepest humiliation and confusion, of the North's greatest shame. William's purpose was to inquire into the future of education and educational books under these changed conditions.

In his methodical, reasonable way he visited schools and legislatures, interviewed governors and teachers, listened, collected information, committed to memory every detail of what he saw and heard. He came north to Cincinnati after a tour that lasted several months and told his story to the publishers. "For days he held his listeners spellbound." One of them later said he "never heard a more interesting tale." Unfortunately no one wrote it down.

The old professor "had made no notes, but he never hesitated for a name. He repeated conversations with unquestioned accuracy and described with humor the gross ignorance and brutality of some of the Southern legislators, the looting of the capitol at the end of the session, the indirect robbery . . . the reversal of all the conditions of life, and the growing unrest of the men who had heretofore been the rulers.

"It was such a picture as at that time no Northern paper would have dared to print — it was the truth."

However dark the political prospects of the South might be, the publishers of the *Readers* were not downcast by William's report. They knew that in any event Southern children would need schoolbooks, probably more than before, and they set to work on the Southern market with extraordinary success.

William himself was profoundly disheartened. He was a friend of both the Southern white and the Negro. What he had seen on his tour led him to think the problem of their future relations almost insoluble.

At the University of Virginia, too, conditions were depressing and were not likely to improve for many years, more than he had left to live. The authorities had no money, and the students lived and worked in Spartan simplicity. Many of them were young soldiers of the Confederate army, returned with broken health, heirs of a Lost Cause.

Even the professors received hardly more than a living. Lack of creature comforts and diminution of income never troubled William. And the publishers of the *Readers* had begun to pay him a small annuity, as their postwar profits soared. He was able to lay aside for a rainy day and to help the needy of Charlottesville, white and colored. Laura was thrifty, and their tastes so simple.

But it hurt him to see "his dear boys" working under a sense of defeat and with a cloud of uncertainty over their future. The way of life that they and their forbears had loved and fought for was ended forever. William, though he lived to see the worst phase of Reconstruction ended, was denied a glimpse of the New South or a rejuvenated university. He found his consolation in books, nature, and the society of his students. To wander in the surrounding woods and hills with one of his students, expatiating on the beauty and harmony of natural law to an attentive young listener, was his favorite diversion.

"All nature was to him the expression of the Divine Thought." The inexplicable and implacable cruelty of nature he seemed not to see, or perhaps he saw beyond. Apparently his complacent faith in "Special Creation" and "Innate Intelligence" never wavered.

To the last he remained a great teacher. Though he dealt with the most abstruse of subjects, he taught "with the simplicity of a child, the precision of a mathematician, and the authority of truth." He rarely flunked a student at finals, not because he was lenient in marking but because he taught with extreme clarity, and the pupil grasped the essentials as he advanced from day to day.

William lectured in the oval east basement room of the large Rotunda, standing on a little platform about a foot high just inside the entrance door. Promptly, when it was time for the students to be seated, he would enter, step up on the platform, arrange his books and notes before him on the pulpit-like stand, and then very deliberately look over the class to see that all were seated and ready to hear. On dark afternoons his lecture stand was always lighted by two green-shaded gas jets set well to the front and on either side of him. If a laggard came in, the doctor would say nothing, but he would pause in the lecture, look over his spectacles at him, and follow him with his accusing eyes until the offender was seated.

His indifference to dress made him a quaint figure. His clothes, though wonderfully neat, were the most old-fashioned ever seen outside a museum. His high linen collar was surrounded by a voluminous black stock, and he wore knee breeches, low-buckled shoes, and silk stockings long after these were quite out of date. At last he reconciled himself to trousers, but he used to conduct his Sunday-morning Bible class in a dark-blue coat with brass buttons, cut something like the present evening-dress coat and known from its shape as a "shadbellied coat."

Tradition varies as to whether William's hair was red or black. But the last of his students to remember him testified that in his old age the Professor's hair was so thin the color was quite imperceptible. His faded locks had receded from his wide brow, leaving his head, except for a fringe, bare as a dome. His shaggy brows hung like mossy crags over his deep-set somber eyes. His cheeks and mouth lacked the fashionable adornments of a beard or "burnsides."

The darling project of William's last years was the writing of his *Magnum Opus*, a ponderous "Mental Philosophy" in four volumes to embody his teachings of fifty years. Only the first volume of this philosophy was published before his death. The others are preserved in manuscript in the museum of McGuffey mementos at Miami University, unread and forgotten, beside the *Readers*, his youthful labor of love, still as fresh and entertaining as when they were written.

William's last lecture was one he gave for the schoolchildren of Charlottesville in May, '73. After delivering it, he was taken ill, with "congestion of the brain," the same ailment that had carried off Daniel Drake. The diagnosis must have covered a multitude of maladies. William failed to rally, and word went around the campus that good "Old Guff" was dying.

The end came on a Sunday evening, at sunset, an evening so full of peace and beauty that it seemed a pity to die. But he was willing to go. He was tired. He had had enough. Laura held his hand, and he gave her last messages for his daughters.

But it was to "the boys" that he longed to speak once more. The old Scotch Puritan welled up in him, strong in death. He wanted to preach, to teach, "to straighten out the crooked sticks" one last time.

William was seventy-three when he died, and his life had covered almost exactly the first three quarters of the nineteenth century. Memorials in his honor were read at various colleges, the Virginia faculty went into a thirty-day period of mourning, elegies and eulogies appeared in newspapers and magazines, and Virginia and Ohio competed for the privilege of burying him. Virginia won, and later named a college hall and a school after him.

The widow clothed herself in heavy weeds and wore them to the day of her death — on the street a black bonnet with a long crepe veil that reached to the hem of her trailing black dress, most unbecoming to her complexion, but Victorian proprieties had to be observed.

William had left Laura very comfortably off, provided she was careful, and she had always been that. She went to live with her spinster sisters, who kept a private school in Charlottesville. One summer they all three made a tour of Europe. William had never been abroad.

When Laura died she was buried in the university cemetery, beside her husband, with a monument half as high as his.

Harriet, the first wife, slept among her own people in Ohio, where she had once been young and beautiful and passionately loved.

William's fame spread gradually. The *Readers* did it. The time came when Miami University established a museum where every belonging of his that could be collected is reverently cherished.

But William has a living shrine, such as only legend sets up, in the hearts of millions of old schoolboys and girls. About the turn of the century, when the *Readers* were going out of use, a remarkable revival of historical interest in them began to spring up all over the country. Men and women who had been children in the 1850's, 60's, and 70's had reached the sentimental age. Their schooldays assumed a halcyon glow, and they began to unearth from attics and the top shelves of bookcases certain old dog-eared school Readers. "McGuffey Reunions" were held, and "McGuffey Societies" sprang up in Chicago, Indiana, Ohio, Virginia, and other parts of the Middle West, the South, and the Far West, wherever there were people who had been brought up on "McGuffeys." And apparently every public-school child in America had studied them, with the exception of those in exclusive little New England, where the *Readers* were never used.

XV

Elegant Alexander was sixteen years younger than rugged William and outlived him twenty-three years. He never wrote any more schoolbooks or books of any kind. It rather bored him to talk about the *Readers*. He always regarded his share in their production as a bit of youthful literary hack work done to oblige his brother. He used to say that at least ten millionaires had been made out of the books. But he had never needed money. Many of the millionaires were his good friends, and some of them his life-long clients.

With Elizabeth's inheritance from her father, Dr. Drake, and Alexander's flourishing practice, the Cincinnati McGuffeys were very well off and lived in a large, easy way. Elizabeth had developed into a forceful woman. She was sociable, like all the Drakes. Alexander, a true McGuffey, tended to be a recluse. His home was his castle, and he spent his leisure hours poring over dictionaries in four languages.

His wife would have liked to study with him, but she was too much occupied with her never-ending stream of babies and the care of two houses, for Alexander had bought a country place on the Little Miami River, forty miles from Cincinnati, and employed a German farmer to work the land.

At "Oakwood" produce flowed into the kitchen faster than it could be used, though the recipes in Elizabeth's cookery book (Miss Leslie's, published in Philadelphia, 1837) called for huge quantities of butter, eggs, fruits, and game. Early American cooking was anything but stingy. Her servants toiled early and late, and Elizabeth herself was seldom idle. She washed and dried the porcelain breakfast cups, gathered fruit, arranged flowers, cut the sugar loaf, sorted the linen, and with the long wooden spoon sampled the "sweetmeats" and cordials always bubbling in great kettles at the back of the kitchen stove.

At sundown a long table would be set for supper under the oak trees. All their lives Elizabeth's children remembered the picture their mother made, in her crisp sprigged-muslin dress and wide straw hat, ladling bonnyclabber, ice-cold from the springhouse, out of a huge crystal bowl, heaping it high with crimson berries and clotted cream, for the long row of young McGuffeys.

There were other pictures they remembered with pain. Their mother in her darkened bedroom, sitting hunched and haggard, her handkerchief pressed to her lips, her soft hazel eyes piteous and beseeching as a suffering animal's. For the babies kept on coming. They were willful, obstreperous children and got on their high-strung father's nerves. And the impact of national events leading up to the Civil War brought him finally to the verge of nervous breakdown.

Alexander's world had been bounded by the walls of home, office, church. He was charitable, devout, an authority on civil and ecclesiastical law, a devoted pater-familias, but the strain of public affairs and politics he had always shunned. War between the states, between blood brothers and fellow citizens, loomed as an unthinkable horror. If the South won, slavery would be extended and two rival nations contend for two irreconcilable ways of life. If the North were victorious, the South would never accept the Negroes as citizens. Alexander's mind dwelt on the hopelessness of the outcome, reeled as before an impasse. At night he could not shut out the nightmarish thoughts. He could no longer work, and in the autumn of 1862 he closed his desk, kissed Elizabeth and the younger children good-by, and with his oldest daughter, Anna, a girl of 18, as companion, sailed from New York for Europe.

It had been the dream of his life to see Europe, but he chose a curious time to go. He avoided England, where upper-class sentiment was pro-Confederacy, and spent a quiet winter in Switzerland, returning home in the spring of '63 with his equilibrium completely restored. He found Elizabeth thin and tired and the national conflict at its most critical stage. In July, at Gettysburg, the tide turned, but the year of '64 saw draft rioting in New York and in Ohio a movement for "Peace at any Price" under the "Copperhead" Vallandigham.

Through it all the Northerners lived in comfort and entertained lavishly. In May, 1864 Alexander and Elizabeth sent out silver-edged invitations for a large evening reception to celebrate the twenty-fifth anniversary of their wedding. A month after the party, Elizabeth fell unconscious in her garden at "Oakwood"; and in September of that year she died, after great suffering, aged forty-seven.

Alexander composed an epitaph:

IN HER WERE UNITED A VIGOROUS AND
CULTIVATED INTELLECT
A GENTLE AND LOVING HEART
INFLEXIBLE PRINCIPLES, STEADFASTNESS IN FRIENDSHIP
UNSWERVING DEVOTION TO DUTY
SHE WAS AN AFFECTIONATE AND DUTIFUL DAUGHTER
A LOVING AND DEVOTED WIFE AND MOTHER
AND
FOR MORE THAN TWENTY-FIVE YEARS
A HUMBLE & CONSISTENT DECIDED CHRISTIAN

Below were added six words that Elizabeth had chosen herself:

"She hath done what she could."

Two years later Alexander married a Miss Caroline V. Rich of Boston. She was a handsome and devoted wife, who gave him six more children.

As William McGuffey had lost his three sons, Alexander's were the only ones in the *Reader* branch of the family to carry on the name. All told, Alexander had fifteen children of whom eleven lived to grow up. This makes William's six, with only two surviving, a puny

Alexander Hamilton McGuffey, 1886.

Cincinnati, 1835, with the Second Presbyterian Church in the background.
Courtesy of The Cincinnati Enquirer

Elizabeth Drake McGuffey. From the painting by Thomas Buchanan Read.

Broadway, looking south from Fourth Street, 1848, then the most fashionable residential section of Cincinnati.

Courtesy of The Cincinnati Enquirer

family for those days. Their other brother Henry, the Kentucky doctor, had ten children by his two wives, and old Sandy had not badly done with eleven. But Alexander holds the family record.

As the waves of postwar prosperity rose higher and higher, Alexander rode along on the crest. Yet his style of living was never ostentatious. After his second marriage he moved from the smoky city to a comfortable mansion on Mt. Auburn, one of the lovely hills that encircle Cincinnati.

"Sunbright," the new home, stood at the end of a short avenue — a cul-de-sac — surrounded by wide lawns and spreading trees. Here the last McGuffey of the pioneer age enjoyed what his ancestors had enjoyed in the wilderness, seclusion.

He never kept a carriage but rode to his office in the poky old horsecar, carrying his green bag with a package of sweets tucked in among the documents, in case he met with youngsters on the way.

He collected original paintings, cut glass, and antique sabers but never too much of anything. He liked room to turn round in, and to spare, no cluttering. He contributed to charity, attended diocesan conventions (he had become an Episcopalian under the influence of his wife Elizabeth), patronized the arts, bought his daughters fine wedding outfits, and started his sons in their professions. When his wife Caroline was ill and longed for the country, he went downtown and bought her a huge easeled painting — too large to go on the wall — a sunlit glade in the woods, vivid and beautiful.

His tastes were unerringly simple and sincere and, throughout the worst period of American taste, he remained untouched by the current fashions of gingerbread architecture and fussy furniture and furnishings. He detested bric-a-brac crammed on what-nots, gilded rolling pins, and all the trash dear to the hearts of the '70's and '80's. He never had a Rogers Group or a Currier and Ives chromo in his house.

At "Sunbright" Alexander's second set of children and his grandchildren played together in the old patriarchal way. "Oakwood" had been sold, and he took his family east every summer to Nantucket, "the Island far out to Sea." There on a high bluff overlooking the Sound, the sea winds blew strong by day and night. But the motto over the big fireplace in Alexander's living room read *Auf der Höhe ist Ruhe.*

Alexander hated to grow old. He was not afraid of death, but his love for beauty and independence was outraged by the thought of decay and disability. The gods allowed him to remain, like his father Sandy, a beautiful old man to the last. As he neared eighty his silvery hair was thick, his eyesight and teeth perfect, and he still carried his head high. His body had always been sound as a nut; it was his shy spirit that had sometimes suffered and let him down.

Even the fortunate Alexander could not escape his share of worries toward the end. It was impossible to control Elizabeth's sons and daughters. They had grown up tall, "cornfed," independent, and gone their several ways. His counsels fell on their ears like sounding brass and tinkling cymbals. Financially he had lost heavily in the depression of '93, and it was impossible to recoup at his age. He had outlived his era, the era of national expansion, easy earning and easy spending, large families and paternal authority.

The sense of these things slipping perplexed him vaguely. He could feel rumblings and creakings beneath the social structure that through his century had reared itself to a dizzy height. Proud and secret, he never complained or questioned, with one exception. He often inveighed bitterly against the growing influence of the press upon the language and the careless writing of reporters. Colloquialisms and slang were anathema to him and William. They had fought a battle against the backwoods vernacular, and purity of speech was more than a hobby with them. It was a passion.

In the spring of '96 the machinery of Alexander's splendid body began to run down. To move only from his bed to the sofa and back, he had to lean on a young shoulder. He was like a tall old oak weakened by the wind that must rest itself on a sapling or fall.

He died at "Sunbright" on the third day of June, meeting with dignity the one indignity he had ever endured.

The *McGuffey Readers* had more influence on nineteenth-century American culture than any other books except the Bible.

To William belongs the initiative and the first four *Readers*. The *Fifth* and *Sixth*, the two most often quoted, most dearly loved, are Alexander's. Both men lived and died quite unconscious of their real contribution to posterity.

Asked at the end of their lives what they had accomplished, they would never have answered, "The Readers." But they might have answered that they had tried to be true to themselves, asked favors of no one, never truckled or compromised. They had kept intact the dearest possession their forefathers had brought over the water — personal independence.

INDEX